DISCOVERING
Many of Life's Mysteries, and Secret's on My own
Life's Journey So Far

PHILIP JOHN NICHOLLS

BALBOA.
PRESS

A DIVISION OF HAY HOUSE

Balboa Press books may be ordered through booksellers or by contacting:

Balboa Press
A Division of Hay House
1663 Liberty Drive
Bloomington, IN 47403
www.balboapress.com
1-(877) 407-4847

Because of the dynamic nature of the Internet, any web addresses or links contained in this book may have changed since publication and may no longer be valid. The views expressed in this work are solely those of the author and do not necessarily reflect the views of the publisher, and the publisher hereby disclaims any responsibility for them.

The author of this book does not dispense medical advice or prescribe the use of any technique as a form of treatment for physical, emotional, or medical problems without the advice of a physician, either directly or indirectly. The intent of the author is only to offer information of a general nature to help you in your quest for emotional and spiritual well-being. In the event you use any of the information in this book for yourself, which is your constitutional right, the author and the publisher assume no responsibility for your actions.

Any people depicted in stock imagery provided by Thinkstock are models, and such images are being used for illustrative purposes only.
Certain stock imagery © Thinkstock.

Printed in the United States of America.

ISBN: 978-1-4525-7423-3 (sc)
ISBN: 978-1-4525-7424-0 (e)

Balboa Press rev. date: 9/18/2013

PREFACE

What lies before you on the following pages of his book, is my personal interpretation of events, that have change my life forever, and has also given my life, a new sense of true meaning in every way. On my Life's journey so far, i have been shown my true purpose for being here on this planet today, and within these last few years of my own life's journey, i have been shown the true wonders, of how magical life can really be here on our planet. I now feel that i have fully awakened from a long deep sleep, that i have been fighting to awaken from, for such a long time. I also feel that i have come to a point in my own Life's Journey, where i must begin to share these truly enlightening secret's, with everyone here on this planet today. My only hope is that the information contained within the pages of this book, will begin to give you the same inspirations, and courage, that i have found on my life's journey so far, hoping that these inspirations will encourage you, to embark on your own life's journey of discovery, beginning to open you up, to the true wonders that life holds for us all here on this planet today, if we are only willing to seek them out.

Introductions

I am going to start this book by explaining a little bit about myself, at the time of writing this book, i have reached the the mature age of thirty nine years, i am a family man, from the United Kingdom, i have two beautiful children who i love with all my heart. At the time of writing this book, my daughter Danielle is thirteen years old, and my son Kyle is eight years old, i also have an amazing wife, she truly is my sole partner in life, and i also love her with all my heart, her name his Wendy. Since leaving school at the age of sixteen, i have tried my hands at a numerous different careers, but never seemed to find the job, that i could say, my heart was in it. After walking out of my last job, i then came to a point of no employment in my early life. Then with a sense of not knowing what i truly wanted to do with my life, or what direction i wanted to take in life, my life seemed to come to a complete dead end. It was then at this point of my life, i decided with great reluctance, to join my farther's family run business. This would be the second time, that i was asked by my father, to join the family run business. The first time, was days after leaving my high school, that first time, i flatly refused his offer. I had already witnessed the consequences of my brother working with my father for many years, these consequences, on occasions caused many family upsets, and also many family arguments. I also felt at that stage of my life, i didn't want to be a part of the family run business. I felt so sure, that i wanted to try and go it alone in the big wide world at large. Unfortunately things never seemed to work out that way, there seemed to be a unseen force at work, driving me back to a career of working within the family run business. I have now worked with my father, and brother in the family run business, for some twenty three years. When i first joined the family business, things turned out exactly the way i thought they would, there was many arguments, and clashes of our different personalities, at some points even leading to physical conflict between us all. But even with these many struggles and upsets, we all seemed to find a inner strength, and courage to carry on working together. I also knew deep down that i truly loved my father, and brother deeply, but the closeness of working with them on a daily basis, and also living in the same house, was a recipe for complete disaster. Even though my mother, and father had been divorced for many years, she was also starting to pick up on the daily upsets, and arguing between me, and my brother Steven, and also my father Kevin. When we all returned home from our working day, i could see the sadness in my mothers eye's, she had a sick sense, and knew before we even said anything, that we had been arguing between each over our work place. I know for a fact, this deeply saddened both me, and Steven, my mother Margaret, as always been a special, and amazing person in both our lives, she means the world to both of us, and we would never intentionally harm her in any way. This was definitely a turning point in all our lives, and in the days, and weeks that followed that day, when we could all see how upset our mother truly was, by our constant arguments, and also our constant physical confrontations between each other at work, we all decided from that day on, our arguing, and our constant confrontations would come to a complete stop. In the years that followed, we all as a family seemed to grow much closer, even though at this point we all started to go our separate ways in life. I think it marked a deeper level of understanding between each other, and also a greater respect for each other to. I myself, found my perfect life partner Wendy, we eventually moved into our own house together, where we would later start our own family together. My brother Steven also found his own life's partner, Pamela, bringing him to the same point of starting his own family to, he also eventually moved into his own house. At this point, unfortunately my mother, and father went their separate ways permanently, but this turned out to be the best for all of us, and also for themselves too. These combined events also made our work life a much better, and also happier place, for all of us to be in. This was my background leading up to my life changing set of events, which started to happen around two years ago. I was like ninety five percent of the population on this planet, living my normal day to day life, going through the motions of working every hour god sends, coming home seeing my family for a precious few hours every day, then eventually getting some much needed sleep, and rest, just to start the same routine all over again, the next day. I seemed to reach a point at this stage of my life, where i hit totally rock bottom, and having a feeling of helplessness inside of myself, not totally knowing, or seeming to understand why i was feeling this way. I think it all started with a build up of the daily stress of running my own family business, and working the many long hours, and late nights, trying to make the business work financially. I thought at the time, this was my only way, to try and make my business a success. But at this point of my life i could start to feel, and also see the many physical effects, of this daily stress building up on my physical body, and also my health in general. This became the point, and the trigger in my life, where i came to the conclusion, that there must be something more to life than this. It couldn't just be, working every hour god sends, and starting the same routine all over again the next day, i felt that life held so much more than this for me. But when i now look back over the past twenty years of my life, i seem to remember asking this same question time, and time again, then i would just put it to the back of my mind again, and carry on with the same daily life routine's. But this time was definitely different for me, the emotions were very strong inside of myself, this time it was something i could not keep in the back of my mind any longer, even though i had tried to on numerous occasions. It was like a constant ache in my mind, and this time it wouldn't seem to leave me alone. I think this is why i have always been interested in the mysterious side of life, trying to answers some of the many unanswered questions, and subjects about human life here on planet earth today. Subject's like space, ufo's, the universe, and many other's, we all seem to be asking the same questions about life, here on this planet, and also the vast universe at large. The question of other life forms living in this vast universe, as always fascinated me, right down to my inner core, just thinking of the many other life forms that may fill our vast universe, seems to fill me with a sense of wonder, and complete happiness inside. I seem to be drawn to the many great secrets about life itself, and the true understanding of who we really are, in this vast cosmos. Even though i have always enjoyed watching many of the new forward thinking documentaries on our tv screens today, and some of them, have even tried to answer some of these difficult, and awkward questions about human life itself. But i feel that they have always fallen short in the many areas of explaining human beings, as a whole, unable or just unwilling to tackle some of the more deeper mysterious issues of human existence itself. I believe that we have not even begun to scratch the surface of the deeper area's of human existence itself, but i do feel, at this point in our human development on this planet, we are as a species, beginning to ask these very important questions. These important questions are now being ask, by the majority of the people on planet earth, instead of the minority of people on planet earth. This new, and important awareness of who we really are, is beginning to sweep over all of humanity, we as the dominant species of this planet, are now beginning to look into every area of our existence. I feel that the number of people on this planet, who are now beginning to awaken to these new, and fascinating facts, about human life, is now growing greater on a daily basis. I feel now at this point of my life, i have also joined their growing ranks, embarking on a my own quest for deeper knowledge, and understanding of who we really are. This is where i believe my life's journey truly began, with a passionate belief, that there is so much more to our lives, here on this planet, than just existing, to survive through our day, to day life. After asking these same questions over, and over again in my head, i came to what i call, a cry for help. I have never had any religious background, or have i ever gone to church, but i felt i needed to asked God for his help at this point in my life. I only asked him once, and then i left it at that, after weeks of nothing more than my usually daily life, and the endless routines contained within it, late one night while i was surfing the internet, i seemed to stumble across a internet page, it just seemed to pop open on to my web browser, and i am not even sure to this day, how i arrived onto this web page, but i am so glad that i did. After i started to read the page, it turned out to be a sort of self help program, written by a man called Dr Robert Anthony. This was the first time, that i had come across, or read anything about these self help programs, regarding human development. I then continued to read further down the web page, and i have to honest here, i nearly closed the web page down, on numerous different occasions, thinking this material definitely was not for me. But there was something inside of me, that wouldn't let me close the web page down, i cannot really explain the feeling i had, it was like a gut instinct feeling, that i needed to read the full web page that lay in front of me. After reading the entire contents of the web page, i felt i needed to find out much more about this mysterious self help program, that claimed to change many areas of your life, from your health, to your wealth. This internet self help program, turned out to be the first program that truly opened my eyes to another part of ourselves which many people on our planet today, still know nothing about. After deciding to purchase the online version of the course, which included many downloadable audio files, and also an amazing wealth of online access to many different help files, and also personal contact information for Dr Robert Anthony himself, if it was felt that it may be needed by the student, at any time during the course. After a short study of the information contained within the online course, i then felt i was ready to start using the course instructions immediately, at first i began the course, with a lot of skepticism inside of myself, but i also held a great sense of excitement about the many possibilities, and also the many outcomes of using this online course, that i felt i had just stumbled across. I had not felt this excitement inside myself for many years, so i began to follow the simple step, by step instructions included with the online course. The main part of the course was the downloadable audio files, that i put straight onto my iPhone, so i could listen to them anywhere, and also at anytime, when i had a spare minute or two. After listening to the many audio files contained within the online course, i completed the full online course in only a few weeks time. On the completion of my online course by Dr Robert Anthony, i immediately started to change my complete outlook on life. I also started to implement the many new life changing suggestions contained within the online course, by Dr Robert Anthony. Within just a month of using this life changing information, i started to see amazing new things happening in every area of my life. When i reached the mild stone of three months of implementing the many new changes within my life, this i feel was the point where i truly started to turn the corner in every area of my life. These many new understandings about life, have sent me onto an amazing, and also life changing journey, which i am still on, to this present day. To date this journey so far as filled my life, with happiness, health, joy, faith, abundance, and so much more. This has now brought me to a point were i feel, i have to share this truly amazing, and also life changing information with as many people as possible from around this wonderful planet. Even though i have no experience in writing books of any kind, i feel as though this is my best way, to tell as many people as possible, about my many life changing discoveries. I feel that i must spread this truly valuable information, that i have encountered along my own life's journey so far. I also feel that i want to share this knowledge with everybody i possibly can, with the hope in my heart, that it will also change the life of every reader of this book, for the better, just the way it has done for my own life. I feel at this point in time, the majority of the human race is in a sort of conscious sleep, but i have hope in my heart, that we are all slowly beginning to awaken from it. I also believe the next few years, will mark a great turning point in human history, and also our conscious evolution on this planet. It will bring humanity much closer, than ever before, it will also give us the many answers, to the many true mysteries, and meanings about human life here on this planet. I also believe we will all start to discover our true purpose for being here in this vast universe at large. I now know at last in my life, i have started to find the answers, to some of the many questions i have been asking myself, over the past twenty or so years of my life here on this planet. I feel that humanity as a whole, is also asking the same questions, we all seem to be searching for same things. We need the answers to the many hidden secrets, and great mysteries within our selfs. These great words of wisdom below, seem to sum up exactly how i feel at this point in my life.

AT FIRST I WAS BLIND, BUT KNOW I CAN SEE.

CHAPTER 1

The Awakening

Has i explained in my introduction section to the book, my journey started with my constant question to myself, about my current life circumstances. Constantly thinking, wanting, and knowing that there was so much more to our lives, than what i was currently experiencing now. I by no means had a bad life, i have a lovely wife Wendy, and i also have two beautiful young children Danielle, and Kyle. I have a successful family run business, repairing motor vehicle's, i am able to pay all my bills and still have money left over to spend on the many luxuries that me, and my family wanted in our lives. To many people this may seem like the perfect life, and in many ways it was. I knew that many people around our planet today, were struggling just to live their daily lives, battling just to find food, to feed their hungry bodies, on a daily basis, also trying to keep their families safe from harm's way. But there was still something missing in my life, many people will think i am being very selfish, and ungrateful for what i already have, and i should be happy with what life as already given to me. I feel that i must stress at this point here, that i am truly grateful for everything i already have in my life, and i always have been, and at first i was very happy with my life, i was also very grateful, and content with every area of my life. I am also not oblivious to the fact, that many areas of our planet today, are filled with people who are starving, and being killed on a daily basis, and are also living in terrible poverty. But i feel this fact as just made me more, and more determined to answer this burning question, which i have been carrying inside myself for so many years. After six months of implementing the things i had learned from the online course by Dr Robert Anthony, i started to notice other little changes in many areas of my every day life. I started to notice that my general emotions felt much better than they had ever done before this point, i also seemed to have much less mood swings, it felt like i was handling stressful situations much better than i had ever done before this point in my life. I had a new feeling of inner joy, that seemed to come from deep within myself. My energy levels also seemed to soar to new heights. The many problem's that used to happen at my work place with my family, and workmates all seemed to come to a complete stop. All the jobs in my garage workshop seemed to be going much better than usual, well ninety percent of the time anyway. We even started to finish work much early than we had ever done before. Only a few months before this point, we would work till very late in the evening, sometimes even past 8.30 in the evening. The funny thing is, the business seemed to be running much better, and much more efficiently than it had ever done before this point in time. The best part of all, we were working less hours, and we were still taking much more money than we had ever done in our many years of running the family business. We just seemed to be getting more, and more customers through our doors, but we wasn't doing any extra advertising or anything different at all. We found this new business success very unusual, because at this point in time, the country and the world at large, was in a state of deep recession. Many of the other local garages in our area, were finding that their businesses where starting to slow down, this was totally the opposite of what we were finding with our business. These strange new events seemed to encourage us all, giving us a new sense of inspiration, and wonder about life. We were all working much less hours, i was spending much more time with family, which i hadn't been doing for a very long time, due to the many commitments of running my own family business. These new developments in our lives, where making both me, and my family feel much more happier with life as a whole. My health also felt much better, than it had done for a long time. At this point i knew something great was happening in all our lives, this new information, and knowledge which i had come across, had the power to change all of our lives for the better. I also started getting much more free time to myself, i feel every person needs this, at some time their life. This special time alone, gives you time to reflect on where you really are, in your life, and also what you really want deep down from your life. The one strange thing that kept playing around in my head, was the fact we seemed to being doing much less work, doing much less hours than we had ever done before, but the fact still remained, the business seemed to be booming, and our bank account also showed or new found success, how could this be. It seemed like some sort of miracle, i feel it was the miracle of self belief. I carried on using the information contained within the online course by Dr Robert Anthony, and even more little things started to happen, and appear in my daily life. My relationships with my children, and especially my wife Wendy was getting better, and better by the day. In fact, all of my relationships seemed to hit new levels of understanding, and lovingness. I eventually hit a point, where i was thirsty beyond words for more knowledge regarding these new, and fascinating subjects in my life. Then one evening while i was browsing the apple iTunes store on my iPhone, i unexpectedly came across an audio book called the Secret by Rhonda Bryne. I can now say with all my heart, this was no accident, and it has also changed my life beyonds words forever. At this point i feel i must Recommend that you either buy this amazing book, or download the audio version of this book, and read it three, or four times so it imprints its self in your consciousness, and also your subconscious mind. At this point in my life's journey, i

3

feel i was guided to the audio version of this book, because of my poor reading skills at this time. Up until this point in my life, i had never read much at all, and i didn't have a great reading skill either. I felt i didn't have the patients to read books in general, and to be honest, they didn't really interest me, at this stage in my life. So at this point, i decided to download the audio version of the book by Rhonda Bryne, straight to my iPhone. From the very first lines of the book that were spoken by Rhonda Bryne her self, i was immediately captivated, with what Rhonda Byrne was saying. Even though this information was all new to me, it was like i already knew all about it, and i was just being reawakened to it. I couldn't stop myself from listening to the audio book, over the coming weeks, i must of listened to it, some seven, or eight times, in just one week alone. I started to listen to the book, at every spare moment i got. I just wanted to go over every point checking, and clarifying every little detail, just to make sure i understood everything i was listening to. This special book, brought me to a even greater level of understanding about this world we live in, and our roll within it. With these many new understandings about life, i have now gone on to read a further fourty or more paper back books to date. I have also listened to many more audio books. Just this one fact alone truly amazes me. Within the last two years of my life, i have developed a new, and overwhelming passion for reading, coupled with a unquenchable thirst for knowledge and truth. Within the next chapters of this book, i will be sharing with you, my amazing life's journey so far. In the last two years of my life, this journey so far as truly filled my life with wonder, and amazement, and as also given, and shown me many miracles along the way. I will also be sharing with you, the tittles of the many books, which i have read along my life journey so far. I feel that many of these books are relevant to the subjects mentioned in here within my book. I also feel that i was guided to each one of these books, just at the right time in my life's journey. I also feel that they have all played their own individual part, in helping me greatly on my life's journey of new discoveries so far. In this amazing book the secret by Rhonda Bryne, the most important thing i learned from the very start,

4

was your minds thoughts coupled with a true heart's desires, which basically means something you feel very passionate about. These two simple things coupled together, can actually change, or manifest real things into our physical world around us. The first time i heard this statement, i thought this must be some sort of joke. If this was really true everybody would be doing it, we would all have huge houses, fast cars, huge bank accounts etc. This may sound ridiculous, and at first it did to me. I just couldn't seem to get my head around it, i must have listened to the book four or five times before the words even started to sink into me. I am a very skeptical person by nature, and i like to see the evidence with my own eyes, before i believe anything. But i had a feeling, deep inside my self, i just felt there was something to all of this. I then knew at that point, i was at the beginning of something, i had been searching for all my life.

CHAPTER 2

My first use of the Law of Attraction

With great excitement, i immediately started to apply this new knowledge, to every area of my life. I first started to use it on the smallest of things in my life, simple little things, like asking for my children to be good, and behave them selfs. I'll be honest, i didn't have much luck there. I knew from the very start, that you could never try to enforce your will on anybody else, this would only cause negative energy, and would never work out the way you wanted it to. I then started to create a new, and positive energy for my work environment, i started to visualize all of the daily difficult job's in the work shop, going smoothly, and effortlessly, instead of the usual car workshop chaos. At first i seemed to be getting mixed results, things definitely started to improve, we would still get the odd problem or two, but the general daily problems of running a vehicle repair workshop, seemed to start slowly disappearing. It felt like things were starting to run much more smoothly in every area of my life. There was a definite change happening around me, i could sense it, even my family, and work colleagues were all picking up on it to. It was starting to create a totally different atmosphere, within my home, and also my work environment. With these new successes in my life, coupled with my earlier success from the online course with Dr Robert Anthony, i seemed to be reaching new heights of happiness, and discovery in my life. At this point, i could also sense something else happening in my life, i could not really explain what it was, but i knew there was unseen force all around me. This unseen force was influencing, and instigating these many new changes, that where taking place within my life. These many new feelings inside myself, just seemed to spur me on even more, pushing me to apply it to many more area's of my daily life. Weeks later me, and my brother Steven were looking for two new cars to lease for our company. The current lease contract was about to end, and with the current economic climate our current lease company, had no new deals to offer us. We tried numerous other lease companies, but we just could not seem to find the right deal we both wanted. Another few weeks went by, but we still hadn't found any new lease deals for our company. I then decided to apply my new found knowledge to help us with this problem of finding two new lease cars for our company. Many months earlier, me and my brother Steven had both set our hearts on getting two new chrysler 300c's, after we had both seen one driving around our local town. These cars looked amazing, but none of the lease companies we had contacted, even had them on their stock list's. So i went to work, not even mentioning this to my brother at all, fearing that he would think i had lost my mind completely. I started of with visualizing me and my brother Steven driving the two chrysler 300c cars. I continued this for about a week or two, i even placed pictures around the garage of the cars themselves. I really believed one hundred percent that we would have a lease deal very soon. At that point i had no doubt whatsoever in my mind, that this would happen for both of us. Within ten days, i had received an email from a company, that we had never dealt with before, or had we ever enquired about leasing cars from them. In their email, they were offering an unbelievably deal on two amazing black chrysler 300c's, the exact colour we both wanted, wow!!!!!. I contacted the company straight away, and within one hour of contacting them, we had secured two new lease deals, on two black Chrysler 300c's. I even ask the company how we had gotten onto their mailing list, and to my amazement, and also hers, we wasn't even on their mailing list, and she couldn't explain how they had come to email us this amazing offer. At first i thought to myself, could these amazing set of coincidence's, really be happening because of my new manifestation power's. This is the problem when you first start to use this great power inside of yourself, you start to wonder, and question was that really me doing that, or was it just a amazing set of normal coincidence's. But the more i put this truly magical power to work, and i seen the results with my own eyes, i then truly started to believe with all my heart, that it would work, and it did work. What i started to quickly learn, and realize from the very beginning of using this amazing power, that lies within us all, was the things you wanted to manifest into your life, may not totally work out the way you thought they would. I could never have predicted the many strange sets of circumstances that would lead me to the many things, i wanted to manifest, and also create within my life. Many of the things i thought i wanted to manifest, and also have in my life, turned out to be, the exact opposite of what i thought i truly wanted to have in my life. What i am trying to say here is, this strange, and unseen power, seems to know what i wanted in my life, before i even knew it my self, it seemed to know the exact thing i was really searching for in my life. What i eventually realized was, the many different things i wished to manifest into my life, may never actually manifest the way i thought they would. At first i would think of these many different outcomes, in a disappointed, and failure state of mind. But i would later come to realize that just around the corner, something much better would always manifest, and appear into my life. Something that i could of never predicted in my wildest dreams. After truly reflecting on these new, and unexpected outcomes, i would then truly realize that these new, and different outcome's was in my best interest's after all. I would also notice that these outcomes, would also take into account the many other people, that was also around me, at that point in time. I then knew, and felt at this stage, that i had truly found an amazing secret, to a part of life, that had been hidden from me until this point in my life. It started to fill my life with joy, and complete happiness again, it was like being a child all over again. I was discovering a new, and hidden world that was filling me with a sense of true mystery and expectation. I felt like i wanted to tell every body about it, most of all my family. But unfortunately at this time, i still wasn't sure how to tell them about these many new discoveries, that where now appearing into every area of my daily life. This was mind blowing stuff, and i could not just come out with it, and tell anybody, they would just think, and say i had lost my mind. I feel like i need to use this power many more times, to build up my knowledge of this truly amazing, and fascinating subject. Maybe then i could spread this powerful information to as many people as possible, including my family, hoping that they could also use it in their own lives. My thirst for more information, and knowledge was growing on a daily basis, i felt like a sponge, soaking up every little bit of information that i came across, in my daily life. I then learned that Rhona Bryne, had released another book called The Power. I was so excited by this news, i immediately downloaded it from the iTunes store, then loaded it, straight onto my iPhone. At this point, i also bought both the hard back copies of The Secret, and The Power, and as well as listening to the audio versions of both books, i also read both the hard back books in a matter of days. The new book The Power, again filled me with joy, and happiness, i also felt a great inner sense of knowing. The Latest Book The Power clarified a lot of what the original Secret book had already said, but it also went much further in areas of what science was now saying about these undiscovered, and hidden subjects. It also showed me, how i could use this special knowledge for my bodies own health issues. Again i just went through every little detail, just to clarify every point. With these many new understandings about how life really worked, i really felt like i had won the lottery jackpot. I truly felt on top of the world, this was what i had always been looking for, the treasure at the end of the rainbow. What these two books also helped me to realize in my life, was the fact that i was already truly blessed, in every area of my life. These two amazing book's awakened me to powerful emotion of gratitude. They began to stir my inner senses, and awaken me to the true feelings of gratitude, gratitude for the many things that i already had in my life. At this point i began to feel grateful for everything in my life, including my family, my friends, my health, and also my financial security in life. I had a feeling inside of myself, a feeling of having everything i could ever want in my life, or ever need in my life. I started saying thank you for every little thing that i had in my life, even down to the food, i was eating on a daily basis, and also the water i consumed every single day of my life. I felt that up and till this point in my life, i had just taken all of these things for granted, without even a single thought of how all of these life giving, and also life sustaining commodities had been brought into my life. I felt that i had not even given a single thought about how many people had worked so very hard to bring all of these life saving commodities into my life. I even started to say thank you for all of the things i used in my every day life, i said thank you to all of the utilities companies for providing the water, electricity, gas, where before i had always complained about their prices and service's. But now i was seeing all these things in a total new, and different light. My thank you's never stopped there, i said thank you for my car's, my shoes, the clothes i worn every day, thank you for my healthy body, thank you for my family. I think you get the picture, i said thank you for absolutely everything. The effect of this on my life, was nothing short of miracle. My life started to flow like a clam river, there were no more ripples in the river anymore, and if there was, i handled them with ease, and with a sense of total calmness. This little change in my awareness, and the simple statements of saying thank you, for the things we all take for granted in our every day lives, as truly changed my life beyond words. You will be truly amazed at the change in your own life, just by doing this simple little act. Many other things, seemed to follow of the back of this simple little act of saying thank you. I seemed to find a new found respect for everyone around me, i also started to give out more love and joy, and i also started to receive it back in my own life. These new feelings of love and joy in my life, began to fill me with great feelings of happiness, and gratitude for everything that i had in my life, especially for the people who was the closest to me. To my amazement, i even started helping my wife with the many different jobs around the house, including the dishes, the cooking, the ironing, and the cleaning, in fact all of the daily things that my wife has had to do on her own for such a long time. I am truly ashamed to say that i had never really help my wife, with the many daily household chores, before this point in our fifteen year relationship together. I had some crazy, and ignorant notion inside my head, that because i was the main money earner in the household, i had the right to sit on my back side after work, and have my wife do all the cooking, washing, ironing etc. The fact that i seemed to forget, or wanted to forget for my own personal, and selfish reasons, was that my wife Wendy, also worked very hard in a full time job, and was also tired when she had finished her day at work to. This marked a turning point in my way of thinking, towards my position, and the many responsibilities in my family life. From that day on, i made it my new mission in life, that i would help my wife with everything i possible could, including all of the many household duties, and also with the bringing up of our two wonderful children, Danielle, and Kyle. I cannot begin to explain how great this as turned out to be for our relationship as a whole. Up till this point in our relationship, i did not even know how far we had drifted apart in our many years together. I now realized that i had been taking Wendy for granted, without even a second thought for any of her feelings. This new sense of awareness, that was enlightening my life in every way, was not just giving me the true meaning of life, it was opening a door way to another world, with a better way of living, and understanding.

It was also starting to show me how we are all one in this world, i now knew that we must treat each other with great love, and understanding, also giving the greatest of respect to our fellow human beings on this planet. This new understanding about life, that i had discovered, really did make a world of difference for both me and my family. It seemed like before, i couldn't see what i was doing wrong in my relationships, i was only seeing what i wanted to see. At this new turning point in my life, i was starting to pick up on the many new things surrounding my daily existence. Before this awakening point in my life, i feel i have been missing all of life's guidance, or maybe before, i just didn't care what life was trying to show me. I came to understand that my old way of seeing the world, was causing me to miss the very special things that was surrounding me, in my daily life. These new feelings, and senses seemed to be giving me enormous amounts of energy, with a feeling of inner satisfaction. My overall health, and well being was also greatly enhanced, i seemed to be smiling from inside of myself. Obviously at this point, every body around me, including my friends, and family began to see these many changes within me. It was hard for anybody not to. At this stage of my journey, both my family, and friends didn't really understand what was going on in my life, and they couldn't quite explain my new state of being. Some of my family, and friends, were even quite concerned, others seemed to accept that what ever was happening to me, was for the better good of all. My new found energy, and zest for life, was giving me the chance to spend much more precious time with my children. Before this point i felt i neither had the time, or energy to do so. I felt i was on a role with life, i couldn't see the negative side of anything, i was so positive about everything in my life. To a lot of people around me this was getting quite annoying, and i could see a sort of anger, and announce building up within their eyes. I think they couldn't understand what was happening to me, at this point of my life, i was even amazing myself with my new state of positivity for life. At certain points when i was with different people, they started to resent me being so happy and positive towards life, and other human beings in general. Even though at this point, i wanted to tell everyone about my new found secret, i felt inside that this was not the right time to do so. I have got to be honest, i was only just getting to grips with these many new enigmas in my life, and the thought of having to tell everybody else about these strange new events in my life, was making me feel foolish, and thinking thoughts of they will think i am totally crazy, and i had lost the plot. I knew that they wouldn't understand me, i didn't really know how to tell them about these many new events in my life anyway. The only thing that i was sure of at this time, was the need to find out more information to clarify my new findings about this amazing new life. I also knew at this point, that there was no going back to my old way of living my life, these new understanding about life, would make that totally impossible for me. I had embarked on a journey of no return, this change inside of me, was permanent, and it was defiantly here to stay.

CHAPTER 3

Gathering More Knowledge

T he next thing i knew, i needed to do, was find out more information through the reading of many more books, and also through searching the vast library of internet sites, that seemed to cover these new, and fascinating subjects, in my life. The wealth of online information was amazing, it seemed that there was a growing number of people around our planet, also traveling on their own life's journeys. It was definitely looking like the whole planet was going through a sort of conscious change in their awareness. These many new internet sites that i was visiting for help, and information. Started to point me in new directions, that i felt i needed to go. I also went to my local water stones book store, this was the first time ever for me. It felt quite strange at first, because i had never been a book reader, up until these last few months of my life's journey. But after about five minutes of being inside the book store, a sense of peace, and calm came all over my entire body. My senses seemed to become heightened in their awareness, i could strongly smell the many books, that filled the store's shelf's around me.

The smell from the books, seemed to fill the entire air, that surrounded my body. I felt immediately at home in this new alien environment, something had definitely changed inside of me, here i was inside water stones book store, and i felt completely at home, with it all. At that point i felt that i had been a reader of books, all of my life. The most amazing fact to me, was how i seemed to read books now, with great ease, and understanding, it was almost coming completely natural to me. This new thirst for greater knowledge, and understanding, had given me a new way to enjoy, and read books. These new feelings, began to fill me, with a new sense of understanding about my life. I walked around water stones book store, looking at the different sections, and titles that were available. I felt myself immediately drawn, and guided to a section in the store called self help. I started to looked around the three or four shelfs that filled this section. Straight away, there were three books that immediately seemed to stand out to me. These three books somehow captured my immediate attention, they seemed different from all of the other books that filled the shelfs of this book section. I am still not sure how these books stood out from the many other books that filled the same shelf's, but never the less these books definitely seemed to stand out to me. I just had a new sense of inner knowing, and guidance, i seemed drawn towards each one of these new books, picking only these three from the many others. I had new feelings of knowing, that these books where the ones relevant to my life's journey, at this point in time. This strange feeling of knowing, was very new to me, knowing, but not knowing, and understanding why i knew. I then picked up the books that seemed to stand out to me, and made my way to the counter to pay for all of them. In the end i ended up with three books in my hands, which were, Barbel Mohr Instant cosmic ordering, The secret within Annmarie Postma, Creative Visualization Shakti Gawain. I immediately started to read them one by one, and soak up all the valuable information, contained inside each one of these truly valuable books. These great books in their own rights, also give me many new recommendations of many other books, that i should read, and discover on my life's journey. There was also a wealth of references,

15

to many new internet site's, for me to look through, and study from. The pattern of being led to books, and new information continued, it seemed again that i was being led to one book, then to another. The next couple of books which came into my life, through a series of coincidental happenings was, The Divine Matrix by Gregg Braden, and The Power of the subconscious mind, by Joseph Murphy. After reading these two life changing books, in an amazingly short period of time, i was truly amazed, by the level of detail, that i had taken in from all of these very special books, that had entered into my life. I seemed to have a great understanding of what the authors of these books where saying in just a very short length of time. I had gathered a wealth of knowledge on these amazing, and fascinating subjects, where only months before this point, i knew nothing about any of them. This new level of learning, was giving me amazing feelings of happiness inside of myself. This was definitely mind blowing stuff for me, and i was finding certain area's of this new information, quite hard to take in. I am not sure in which order i read these fascinating new books, but this did not seem to matter, they all seemed to speak with one great voice of truth. The fact i read them with great interest, and also enjoyment, seemed to be telling me something. I just couldn't seem to put them down, i even started to re-read many of the books that gave me the most enjoyment, and also most inspiration. I was quite shocked with my new found skill, and also my new joy for reading. I know this may not sound amazing to some people, who have always read books, but reading books, and understanding them, was truly a giant leap for me. I then purchased more books, which i am going to mention here, because i feel they played a very important part in my life's Journey, the titles are as follows. The biology of belief by Dr Bruce H. Lipton P.H.D, The deeper secret by Annmarie Postma, and Ask and it is Given by Esther and Jerry Hicks. This is only a few of the titles, that i have read, but it is now unmistakable that i am definitely being led to one book after another, in a unmistakable set of sequences. All these books seemed to point to same thing, but in a round about way, they are all telling the same story, in slightly different ways. When we use or thoughts, coupled with our emotions, and feelings, we truly have the power to change, create, and manifest anything we want, into what we call our physical reality, here on planet earth. THOUGHTS BECOME PHYSICAL THINGS!!!, please remember this simple statement, it will truly change your life for ever, and also for the better. The information given in these two life changing books, The biology of belief by Dr Bruce H Lipton P.H.D, and Gregg Bradens Book The Divine Matrix, is truly amazing. Science now as solid scientific proof, that our thoughts, have a direct affect on the atoms, and partials of matter which surround everything we see, and also cannot see. This matter is what makes everything in our world, from the living things, to the non living things. This only confirmed scientifically to me, what i already knew inside myself, it also clarified what many of the authors of the books, that i had already read along my journey so far, had been saying all along. This new information, i believe is going to bring a new era in human understanding, and evolution on our planet. It will begin to change our views of life itself, and our role in this vast universe. Maybe soon the oldest question of life itself, will be answered in a dramatic way. WHO WE REALLY ARE.

CHAPTER 4

The Power of the Human Mind

I now believe at some point in our lives, we all eventually come to a point, were we need to look inward, and find our own true self. We all seem to be looking for something in our lives, i believe this is where we meet, and also join our life's journey, embarking on a search, for our true life's purpose, the real reason for being here this time around on planet earth. I feel that many people chose to ignore, and forget their true life's quest, and also their true purpose for being on this earthly realm. They become lost in the mayhem of their day to day lives, here in this material world. Many of us, don't even want to look deep down within ourselves, fearing the answers, that they may find, hidden deep within. But i now know and feel, that looking deep with ourselves, is our only way, to begin our life's journey, eventually leading us to the answers to our true destiny's, and purpose, of being here on earth at this time now. I believe now at this point in my life, i have at last started to find these elusive answers to every area of my life. I feel i have now joined this great new era of human evolution on our planet today, leading me into a new awakening of my inner consciousness. I feel truly privilege to be taking part in this new era of human understanding on our great planet today. I believe this new state of human understanding, of who we really are, will begin to heal, all of humanity. Bringing us all much closer together as a species, also helping us to work much closer together in every area of human existence on our planet. This will finally bring the world into a state of much needed peacefulness. It will give us all new levels of understanding each other, we will all start to understand, and embrace our true life purpose's, this time around. We will all come to believe and feel, that what we see with our human eyes, as a physical, and material world, is nothing more than a elaborate illusion, created by our truly powerful minds. The world we truly live in, is a vast invisible energy field, which is affected, and also shaped by our internal thoughts, and emotions. We can literally create, and shape this field to our own advantage, or disadvantage. The implications of this one true fact are truly mind blowing, and once it is truly understood by the reader of this book, it will begin to change your life forever. We literally have the power to change our lives completely, just by using our thoughts, and emotions combined together, WOW!!!. At this point in my life, i have started to truly awaken, and also realize that this mysterious power of thought, and emotions combined, could work on just about any desire i wanted to have in my life. Including my health, wealth, happiness, truly anything i could imagine, or ever dream of having in my life. I am a thirty eight years old, and i have been struggling with hair loss since the age of 24, if you have been through this yourself it can be an emotionally devastating disease, and it can affect you in many different ways, from self a steam, right through to emotional depression. So i knew deep down inside me, that this was one of my true heart desires, that i wish i could fix in some way. I am not saying this is a life threatening disease in any way, and i know that many people just accept the fact there loosing their hair, and get on with their lives, and that's fine. But for some people in life, including myself, it can be a truly devastating time of life. Because of the way i felt about my hair loss, i knew my emotions surrounding the subject was also going to be very strong, and intense, so i decided, i would make this, my first health goal, using this amazing, and powerful knowledge. I then, immediately started picturing my self with a full head of hair again, like when i was nineteen years old, some may call me vein, or even silly, or think its a waste of this amazing power we have inside our self's. But i classed this has a true health condition, that as made me quite miserable, and depressed over the many years of my life. This condition, has also given me a very low self esteem, and also a image of myself, that i didn't truly like, for a long time. Anyway i did this visualization for some weeks with no results at all. Then about one month into these strong visualizations, i received a unexpected email in my inbox at work. It was about hair transplants, and a new generation of technology, that was making it affordable to the larger population. it was also producing new, and amazing results, i will be honest here, it wasn't the solution i was looking for at all, i am not quite sure what i was really expecting to happen. I really thought it may just start growing back on its own again, this may have possibly happened if i had given it more time. But as i later found out in other creative manifestations, it sometimes doesn't work the way you always plan it to, you have got to leave yourself open to the many possibilities, and endless set of different scenario's that can be created by this vast unseen power within us all. The hair transplant was something i had only heard of ten years or so before, but it used to look like dolls hair, and was a very painful process indeed. There was no way, i would of gone through that painful process, and at the end of it all, still look like a dolls head of hair. But this time, there was something different, the technology had advanced greatly in every area. The email that i received at work, seemed to have come from no where, just like the car manifestation, earlier on, in my life's journey. I had never registered with any hair transplant sites, or any other sites about hair loss, in fact i was quite embarrassed by the subject, and i have always kept it to my self. I just had a gut feeling to take a look at this new avenue, that again seemed to come from nowhere, i just felt inside, that i should not dismiss it outright. I started to question, was this really me creating this new reality for myself, with this great new power, and understanding that i had discovered. I first tried to find out where the email had originally come from, i followed the link to the main site, and continued to read about the many new developments in this technology, and also the new techniques that was being used. My excitement was starting to grow, the new techniques were amazing, and the results where also truly outstanding. The site also showed many pictures of their successful procedures, on many different patients. The new procedure basically took healthy follicles of hair, from the part of your head where the hair was plentiful, and then transplanted them back in to the area's where there were no hairs, or very few. With a sense of great expectation, i then contacted the hair transplant company in Harley street London. I immediately made an appointment for a consultation, where i later learnt that their client list included some of the rich, and famous form all over the world. These new findings only made me more determined, and also at ease, with the idea of having the hair transplant. I had the consultation a couple of weeks later, it was my first time in London, i was very excited, and also a bit apprehensive. Here i was in this large beautiful city, all alone. I also knew this was something, that i needed to do on my own, my partner Wendy, and also my family at large, didn't understand my reasons, and also my needs for having the hair transplant. My family never wanted me to have the hair transplant, but it meant a great deal to me, and i knew that i really needed to go through with it. I feel this reality had come about, from my powerful visualizing, mixed together, with my powerful emotions on this subject. After a great, and successful consultation meeting with the hair Doctor at Harley Street, i was booked in for the hair transplant, just before christmas 2010. The day before the surgery i traveled to London by train, because my appointment, was for the morning after, at a very early hour. The next day, with a sense of great anticipation, i made my way to the hair transplant surgery. After a full day of very successfully hair transplant surgery, i left the clinic, and made my journey back home to my waiting family. After the initial healing, and slight pain following the hair transplant surgery, i began to recover very quickly indeed. In only a few months, i began to start seeing, amazing results from the hair transplant. I was beginning to see how dramatic the results was going to be, from my hair transplant surgery, it was going to change my life completely. After a eight month period, i finally got back my full head of thick hair again. This had a dramatic, and also life changing effect on me. The people who were closest to me started saying you look ten years younger, many other different people also commented of how extremely healthy, and vibrant i was looking since my surgery. I also felt much healthier, and happier within myself, i felt i had gotten back my self a steam. This was great because in a matter of six months, i was to be married to my life long partner Wendy. The funny thing was i started to feel young again, i developed a new enthusiasm for life again, which i now know, that my hair loss had taken away from me, somewhere along the line. I wanted to do the things young people was doing again, i started to go out, and mix with people again, i had my confidence back again. It almost seemed has though i was a child inside again, i started to socializing more, and more, which again was something that i felt i had lost a long time ago. This was a new and exciting time for me, and i put it all down to my new found knowledge of this amazing universal power. The greatest feeling which come form all of this, was the power that i could begin to feel inside of myself, i now knew what i had inside me, and i could use it to help change my world for the better. I could also help to share this great, and amazing secret with as many people has possible from around our wonderful planet. It seemed at last that i had truly found the great secret to all life.

CHAPTER 5

The Set Back

Then after all these great new events and happiness in my life, i was hit with a very emotional low point in my life, leading me into a great set back, in my life's journey so far. My dog Jake, who was my true best friend for some seventeen years of my life, was beginning to show signs of illness. He had not been him self for sometime, i could begin to see the difference in his character. Usually Jake was a very active and large hearted character, he was always bursting with large amounts of energy. But in the last six months or so, Jake had seemed to change very rapidly. He had stop being is usual self, at times he even seemed very distant from his surroundings, always wanting to sleep, and he even looking tired within himself. I knew Jake was seventeen years old in human years, and i also knew this was a grand old age for a dog. But the thing that began to scare me the most, was Jake's loss of desire for going out doors, he truly loved being outside, and in that moment, i knew in my heart, that there was something very wrong with him. Jake had always had good health over the years of his life, and he had only ever been to the vets three of four times, in is entire life. But in those few trips to the vet, that jake had encountered through is early life, he had built up a great dislike for going to the vet's. I knew that taking him to the vets, was going to be a very stressful time for him, and with Jake now being seventeen years in human terms, i was very fearful of what would happen to him, and also fearful of what the vet may diagnose. Even though Jake was showing no signs of pain, or great unhappiness, i just felt it was time to see what the problem was with him. I booked Jake in for an appointment at the vet's, one week later. When we both arrived at the vets, Jake was showing is usual signs of fear, but this time the fight had seemed to have gone out of him. In his early days, i would of needed to mussel Jake to have the vet examine him. But this time, i was very saddened to see that all the fight, had seemed to have left him. The vet needed to run a series of tests on Jake, to try and find out what the problem was, this meant that i would have to leave him at the vets all day long, on his own, i could immediately see the fear in his face, as they took him away from me. At that point a dark sense of fear, and sadness engulfed my entire body, i felt as though my life connection to Jake, was beginning to weaken. I knew i needed to compose myself, and be strong for Jake, but it was not easy at all. When i entered my vehicle to drive back to work, i immediately broke down into tears, taking quite a while to calm my self down. Later that day the vet telephoned me, and ask me to pick Jake back up, they said they would speak to me when i arrived at their office. In the back of my mind i felt the worst, but i still hoped for the best outcome for Jake. When i arrived Jake was there waiting for me, with is tail wagging as usual. The veterinary nurse approached me, and ask me to follow her into the diagnoses room. She gently, and politely informed me that jake had large tumor's in his spleen, and also his stomach area. She explained that they could not operate on Jake, they feared that he wouldn't survive the operation, they also felt he was far to old to go through such a traumatic operation. They also stated that even though jake seemed fine at this moment in time, apart from is unusual tiredness, his condition could deteriorate very rapidly. They also said that the tumors would start to spread to all parts of Jake's body. I stood there with Jake in my arms, in a state of complete shock, the colour began to drain from me, my heart was pounding like a drum, and i felt sick right down to my entire being. I started to hug Jake tightly, i didn't want to let him go, and i had a feeling inside me of uncontrollable sadness. I said thank you to the vet, and the nursing staff for all their help, and for their genuine concern about Jake. Me and Jake, then made our way to my van, i continued to carry Jake all the way, not wanting to let him go from my arms. I sat there crying, and completely heartbroken for some time with Jake in my arms, Jake knew completely what was happening to him, and he just kept licking my tears, it was one of the hardest things, i had ever gone through in my entire life. I then returned Jake home to my house, where he could rest, and eat a good meal, which he still thoroughly enjoyed. The next thing i needed to do was inform my partner Wendy, and my two children Kyle, and Danielle. After contacting Wendy at work, she herself broke down into tears, and left work early. I announced the dark news to our two young children at the night time. This deeply saddened all of us, and i find it hard to explain with only words, the feelings that we were all feeling inside ourself's at this time. Even my mother Margaret, and my brother Steven were both deeply affected by the news of Jake's illness. Jake seemed to leave a amazing impression on every body he had encountered through is long, and fruitful life. Just the thought of him not being with us all, was truly heart breaking to say the least. I could start to see in Jake's eyes, that he was beginning to pick up on all of the sadness that was surrounding him. Over the next few months of Jake's life, his deterioration continued, but at this point we never even thought about having him put to sleep, Jake was still in no pain, and he was also eating well, and enjoying all of his food. In desperation, i started to try some of the new healing methods, that i had been learning about, from the many books that i had already read. But as hard as i tried, none of them seem to have any affect on Jake at all. It seemed like his death was already set in stone, it seemed like this was jakes time to go, and nothing was going to change that. It just didn't seem real to me, that my best friend of some seventeen years, was coming close to the end of is earthly life, with us all. Weeks later he took a turn for the worse, and over night he lost his sight completely in both eyes. The vet said the tumors had spread to all parts of Jake's body, and we needed to think about ending his life humanely, before he started to suffer greatly. The words cut through me like a knife, penetrating deep into my inner soul. Wendy and i, had already talked between ourselves about this, we had agreed that the minute Jake started to show any signs of pain, we would have him put to sleep immediately. Then late on a sunday evening, Jake began to deteriorate badly, he was beginning to show signs of severe pain, that we had talked about. I then knew that Jake had come to the end of his earthly journey, here on this planet. I also knew i needed to find the courage for both me and Jake, and also for the rest of my family. The children heartbreakingly said their good bye's to Jake, myself and Wendy took Jake to the vets, where he was humanely put to sleep. I lay on the bed with Jake, when they give him is injection, i never let go of him, and i also looked him straight in his eyes, until he had completely passed to the other side. This was the hardest decision, i had ever needed to make, in my entire life. Myself, and also my family were deeply traumatized beyond words, we never wanted to end Jakes life in this way, i had always hoped, that he would pass to the other side naturally, having a completely peaceful death. This was a very deep blow to me, affecting me emotionally, to the point of physical exhaustion. I couldn't seem to focus for quite a while, a terrible sense of great loss had taken over my life. My partner Wendy, was also taking Jake's loss, much harder than i thought she would have done, i then knew that i needed to support her, and also my family in these darkest of days. With the many new discoveries in my life, i started to challenge many of these dark feelings, and emotions that i held inside of myself, at this point in time. I feel that i was already emotionally charged, by my many new findings about life itself, i felt that i was only beginning to explore some of the many new things that was starting to appear into my daily life. I was discovering many of life's true secrets, but also with a sense of not fully understanding all of them, at this time. These new feelings inside of me, was starting to fill my entire being, with a great sense of helplessness. But all i really wanted to know at this point in time, was Jake safe, and was he also ok, where ever he was. I just could not seem to rest, until i knew for sure that Jake was ok. I again prayed to God for his help, for only the second time in my life. Then a week or so after Jakes death, myself and my family returned home, from a day out, we were just trying to cheer ourselves up, and bring a sense of normality back into our family life. When we pulled into our house driveway, sitting there right in the middle of the driveway, and in the direct path of our car, was a beautiful white dove, just sitting there not moving, and not at all startled, by the presence of our vehicle approaching it. We were all quite amazed, that the dove, didn't just fly away at the site of our approaching vehicle. We all got out of the car, and approached the dove, and we definitely thought it would just fly away, but still it wouldn't move or fly away, even when i approached it closely, and was only inches away from it, still the dove stayed put. I then thought the dove must have been injured in some way, but on further inspection, i could not see any visible signs of injuries to its body at all. We all continued to watch over this beautiful dove, we all knew that our local neighborhood contained many cat's, and with the dove's current circumstances, it would have been a very easy target, and also an easy meal for the many cats that roamed our local neighborhood. But as my daughter Danielle pointed out, it was strange that since we had returned home, we hadn't seen any cats at all, when usually they where always round and about the street at large. We all agreed now was the time to phone the local RSPCA, we knew we wouldn't be able to watch over the dove all night long, and eventually the cats would return and probably kill the dove. It was a further hour, before the RSPCA came to our house to remove the dove. The lady who came from the RSPCA, said she couldn't understand why the dove would not fly away. She then give the dove a full examination, while she was still at our house, and she still couldn't find anything physical wrong with the dove. She also went on to say, that this was a unusual area for this type of dove, she then left, and we all returned to the house satisfied, that we may have saved the dove's life. Even though at this time i didn't think to much of this incident, but in later reflection, i seemed to have a strange feeling inside myself, which i couldn't explain at that time. But over the next few days and weeks, i would also start see white feathers everywhere i went, even on my van windshield in the mornings. Even though at this point of my life's journey, i did not fully understanding the meanings of the dove, and the many feathers, i was now seeing every where i went. The simply fact that i was starting to notice them in my daily life, and also starting to feel their meanings internally, was a big turning point in my life. These strange, and new events, began to activate something deep inside of me. What i am trying to say is, these strange and new events seemed to be sending me on a totally different path, than the one that i had originally started on, at the beginning of my life's journey. This i feel was the start of my spiritually awakening, on my life's journey so far.

CHAPTER 6

The Start of My Spiritual Awakening

I have got to be honest at this point, i do not come from a religious background, or have i ever really studied, or gone to any church services in my lifetime. I would also like to stress the fact that i do not have any great beliefs, or understandings about the worlds different religions, and also different factions. But nevertheless i am beginning to feel a definite change taking place inside of me, which at this stage of my life, i do not fully understand. This was turning out to be quite an hectic time in my life, our wedding day was only three months away, Wendy and i had been planning the wedding for some two years, sorry!!, i mean Wendy did most of the planning for two years. The big day seemed to fast approaching, it was only two months away, and there seemed to be so much to do, before our big day. I was never worried though, Wendy was such a great planner of things, and i think deep down, she throughly enjoyed all of the pressure of planning the perfect wedding day for us both. It must of only been one month before our wedding day, when i suddenly had a feeling of great regret, that seemed to sweep over my entire being. Wendy and i, never planned to have our Wedding ceremony at a church, at the time of planning the wedding with Wendy, i told her i didn't want all the fuss of a church wedding, and could we get married at our wedding day venue, where they could arrange this service for us. At first, i just thought these strange new feelings, that i was getting inside myself, was just my pre-wedding nerves. I tried to shake it off, but the feelings was getting stronger, and stronger by the day. Then only two weeks before the actual wedding day, i sat Wendy down, and told her, i do not know why i am saying this, but i feel inside me, that we need to get married at a church venue. At first, Wendy was in a state of shock, and utter disbelief at what i was saying to her, i think she didn't know what to say at first, then after a long pause, she finally uttered the words, are you mad, we cannot change the wedding venue at this late stage, its impossible. She tried to assure me, that no church in the uk, never mind our own town of warrington, would be able to fit a wedding ceremony in, at such a late stage. I told her, that we would be able to find a church that would marry us, and she would get the church wedding, i know she always wanted. After all the chaos of my startling announcement, we sat quietly and talked about why i had change my mind in such a dramatic way. I wasn't really able to answer that pressing question, i just tried to be as honest as i could with Wendy, expressing to her, this inner feeling of urgency, that was sweeping over my entire body. This great new inner need for us to have a church wedding, was a uncontrollable desire that i could not ignore. At this very point, Wendy also started see for herself, this new change that was taking place within me. The next day Wendy manage to make an urgent appointment with one of our local church vicars. I was quite nervous, and apprehensive, it was only my second or third time inside a church venue, and i had never met with a church vicar before this day. We arrived at the church some twenty minutes early, i hoped that this would give us all a bit of time to reflect, before our planned meeting with the vicar of the parish. Wendy's mother Audrey, came along for some moral support, Audrey had also been married at this church many years before, i actually think it brought back some painful memories for her, she had only just lost her life long partner and husband frank, a year or so earlier. I was truly grateful for her amazing support at this time, in what seemed like our hour of need. Sitting there in silence, in this amazing church setting, i seemed again to get a great sense of inner peace, that engulfed my entire body. I also got the sense that Audrey, and Wendy also found a moment of their own inner peace, inside this amazing church setting. When the vicar 's assistant approached us all, to say it was our turn to ask the vicar our questions, i was extremely nervous, about the outcome, but still i knew this was the right thing to do. After the initial introductions, and brief conversations with the vicar, we then asked the him, can you marry us in two weeks time. He didn't say anything for about a minute, the silence was cutting deep within me, every second of silence that passed by, seemed more like minutes. He then without saying a word, pulled out a little diary, and said what was the date again, Wendy replied in a quite voice, the date was the 13th August, after a short pause the vicar said yes, i can marry you on that day. Even though i knew in my heart, that we would be married at a church, the astonishment of that day being free for us, at one of the busiest churches in the warrington, and also at one of the busiest wedding periods of the year, truly amazed both of us, beyond words. We then had to cancel the old wedding day venue, where we was going to take our wedding vows, but the venue owners were very happy for both of us, and this didn't affect them in any way, we where still having the rest of our wedding day at their venue setting. We then needed to quickly spread the news, that of our wedding day venue, was now going to take place at our local church. After informing our close friends, and also our family members, they were all quite shocked to say the least, they just couldn't believe that we had got in at this amazing historical church in our home town, and also with such short notice. The church was in a truly exceptional location, it was architecturally beautiful, and also boasted a magical outdoor setting. Understandingly, there was usually a very long waiting list to get married at this very special church, with that in mind, i was truly grateful beyond words, knowing that i was about to be married in such a special location, with such a special person. This amazing outcome, was giving me a very warm feeling inside of my self, it also seemed to give me a sense of new excitement for our actual wedding day. I also knew this was what Wendy had always wanted, from the very beginning, i could see this decision had made her extremely happy, i also felt immense relief, and a sense of peace, now that it had been set in stone, so to speak. I then knew at this point in my life, there were external forces at work watching over all of us, in our daily lives, we just need to open our eyes to begin to see them at work all around us. More strange events happened, two days later, we had our last meeting with our wedding photographer, at the meeting she was showing us some of her recent wedding pictures, which she had chosen from her showcase folder. On the last few pictures we looked at, there was a wedding couple releasing a number of doves, at the very end of their wedding ceremony. The very instant i seen this, i immediately said to Wendy we need to have doves at our wedding too, again Wendy said it was to late, but i ask her to trust me again, for the second time. She eventually agreed with me, the next day i searched the internet, to see if anybody offered this service locally, there was only one. I dialed the telephone number on the web site, but no one was there, so i left a long message, explaining our situation, and left it at that. About one hour later, i received a call, confirming that he did indeed have a free booking for that day, and he would be very glad to do it for us. Both Wendy and i where absolutely ecstatic, everything seemed to be going our way, we could not have been any happier at this point in our lives. Our wedding day, turned out to be, one of the best days, of both our life's, everything went like a complete dream, including our special dove release at the end of our wedding ceremony. It was Wendy's true fairytale wedding, and also her life's long dream, i was so happy for both of us, at this point in our lives. The day after our wedding day, we were booked to fly to the magical islands of the Bahamas. Danielle, and Kyle, was also joining us for our special honey moon trip, we could never have left them both behind. We were all very excited about going to these special group of islands, the many pictures we had seen and studied, made it look like a true island paradise, a place of true dreams. When we arrived at the hotel in the Bahamas, our new streak of luck continued to happen. We were all standing at the hotel check in desk, when we were approached by a young lady, who was going to check us into the hotel. She was extremely polite, and also very helpful, she could also see, the true excitement in all our faces. Wendy explained to her, that we had just been married, and this was our honey moon. She then walked over to one of her supervisors, and they started to talk between each other, when she eventually returned, she said i have some great news for you, you are being upgraded to our special five star hotel, called the cove, which would usually cost you eight hundred Dollars per night. We were absolutely speechless by this amazing news, we just couldn't believe how lucky we was, we all felt so grateful, that this beautiful young girl, who we had only just met for the first time, had gone well beyond her normal duties, to help make our trip, a truly unforgettable one. We all said thank you to her, for all the things she had done for us, and wished her all the best for her future. We then got our own private car, with a personal driver to take us to the cove special resort complex. On arriving we couldn't believe our eyes, the place was truly out of this world, it was definitely a true island paradise, we all felt on top of the world. We were then shown to our five star suite, which was breath taking in every way, the view from our room was truly exceptional, it was the place of our wildest dreams. Once we had settled in, and got accustomed to our new luxury surroundings, we all started to relax, and enjoy all of the amazing facilities that was on offer to us. It was about three days into our amazing holiday, when something very strange, and unusual happened to me. This is the first time that i have mentioned this event to anyone, i feel that now is the perfect time to let everybody know about this truly amazing, and life changing experience that i had in the Bahamas. I feel that i must share this experience, with the reader of this book, even if many of you, may find the event very strange, or even to hard to believe. What ever people may think about this event, it was another monumental turning point in my life. The whole event felt so magical to me, and still does, till this very day. I am still not sure of its importance, or significance in my life's journey, but i know that this was a very special sign for me, and just the thought of it, till this very day, gives me goose bumps all over my entire body. The strange event happened about eleven o'clock in the morning, i was laying on the sun loungers, reading a book, that i had brought on holiday with me. On this particular morning, i was laying by myself, and Kyle my son was playing in the pool, not to far away from me. He was excited that he had found a new friend from the United States of America. Wendy, and Danielle had gone for a walk to the small shops, that where situated around the hotel complex. There weren't many clouds in the sky that morning, it was also quite hot, even though it was still early on, in the morning. Then out of the corner of my eye, i could start to see a small bunch of white fluffy clouds coming into my view, they just seemed to appear from no where, which wasn't that strange for this area, weather patterns could change in the blink of an eye. Then something prompted me to look at the clouds again, and in the clouds shapes, there was a perfect face, and i mean a perfectly defined face. It was like looking at a picture of a face, it was unbelievable defined. I don't mean like the little games we sometimes play with our children, trying to pick out shapes in the clouds, this was completely different, i had never seen anything like it. I rubbed my eyes two or three times, to make sure that i wasn't seeing things, that wasn't really there, but it did not matter how many times i rubbed my eyes, the image was still there, and still in perfect definition. I was quite shocked, i looked around for Wendy, and Danielle, but they were still away shopping around the hotel complex. I looked for my son Kyle, i could see him still playing on the other side of the pool, with his new friend. I even looked about for a stranger, to ask them to clarify what i was seeing, but there was only one man, who seemed to be resting, and he may of thought i was completely mad, if i had awakened him, to see a face in the clouds. I stood three looking at the image in complete ore, time seemed to slow down to a complete stand still, even though the whole event, probably only lasted for no more than three minutes, or maybe a few minutes more, the strange sensation of everything around me slowing down, was weird to say the least. I seemed to freeze in a state of suspended animation, then the image just seemed to fade away, has quick as it had arrived. I looked around the whole panorama of the sky, but there was no sign of the image, in fact there was no sign of any clouds what so ever. I lay there in a state of complete reflection on what had just happened to me, what did this mean, was this a sign for me from god, i just didn't know what to make of it. I felt in a state of disbelief of what i had just seen with my own eyes, i could then see Wendy, and Danielle approaching me from the other side of the pool area. I thought quite hard over telling them, about this strange event, but i then decided not to, i didn't know how they would react to this strange set of circumstances. My mind felt in a state of disarray, i just couldn't stop thinking about the implications of this amazing vision, and what it may mean in my life's journey so far. The face that i seen that morning, as burnt a image into my mind, that i can recall at anytime i wish from my memory, it was like the pictures of the gods, we see in the old films, like the god Zeus, and Triton. The vision of this face had a deep affect on me, it couldn't have been something nature had made, its was to perfect and to well defined. I felt i wanted to tell my family about this life changing experience, but something inside of me told me it was a message for me alone, and to keep it to myself until the time was right, to announce it to my family, and then the world at large. To date i honestly don't know what the vision meant for me, but i do believe, and know inside myself, that i changed for ever that day. Something inside of me, awakened and i began to see the world, the universe, and god, in fact absolutely everything in a completely different light. I still question myself every day, asking myself why was i shown this image, was it God trying to give me a sign on this new path of discovery, that i now feel i am on. I sometimes question myself, did i really see that face, or was it a trick of the clouds and sun, but i know deep down that it was a sign for me, and at that point, i had been introduced to a part of my self that only few of us on this planet ever get the chance to know. The whole episode still fills me with a sense of greatness, and knowing, i feel it has change the direction of my life's journey, it as sent me on a totally different direction in my life's quest for truth, and knowledge, in every area of human existence. When i returned home from holiday, it was still there very fresh in my minds thoughts, it must a been a few weeks later, and i was still constantly thinking these events over in my mind. Then late one night i was watching a program on sky tv, and it was about a group of people who think they may have found evidence that the Lost City of Atlantis was true, and it may have been situated in the islands of the bahamas. These fascinating legends, and mysteries have always intrigued me, i continued to watch the program with a sense of great excitement, i am not quite sure why i mention this here, but i feel that i need to, the fact that i had just returned from these magical island, coupled with my life changing vision, while i was there, leads me to believe that my vision has great relevance in my life's journey. Watching this fascinating program began to bring the picture of the face, back into the fore front of my minds thoughts again, it also brought back all of the emotions, that went with this amazing, and magical memory. My body was again filled with goose bumps, and there was a sense of static in the air around my body. I began to think thoughts of, could this face in the bahamas, be connected to Atlantis in some way, and if so, how did it fit in with my life's journey. Some people my think these events are very strange, and they may also think, that i may be loosing my mind in some way, but i assure you, that i am still a well grounded person, and i still lead a normal life with my family. The truth is, i am still not quite sure why all of these many new things are happening to me, but some where inside me, i know this as a meaning to my life's journey. Maybe the meaning of these very strange events, will decide to show their meanings at a later stage of my life's journey, all i know at this point of my life's journey, i have just got to keep myself focused, and grounded, but i must also keep my mind open, to many of these truly magical, and mysterious moments, that life has brought to me, leading me on to a path of true discovery, and wonder, filling my whole being with a new sense of amazement, and thirst for life.

CHAPTER 7

Directions

In the weeks that passed, i seemed to look more inward, i was asking myself many more questions, that i felt needed to be answered. On my return home from what seemed like an unusually long day at work, i was sitting in the usual daily traffic jam, when something caught my eye, on the back of a car window, just in front of me. The sign on the back of the car window, seemed to stand out to me, it was almost like the writing had a sort of illumination glow around it. I immediately felt a inner sense of knowing, that this was a important message for me. The top of the message read, talking with spirits, and stated a reference to a website page, that i immediately typed into my iPhone. Later that evening, i felt an uncontrollable urge to visit the internet site, that i had earlier typed into my iPhone. The web site turned out to be, a spiritual medium who did readings for people, she also learned people in different spiritual practices. At that point, i said to myself, i must have miss read this message, and any meaning it may have had for me, i thought to myself, this is not for me, this sort of thing just didn't feel right for me, and there was no way i was going to see any type of spiritual medium. Even though at this point in my life's journey, my mind was beginning to open up, to new types of thinking, and all different possibilities, about life, i still thought this type of thing, went to far for me. I thought that if i went to see this spiritual medium, my family, and also my friends, would begin to think i had definitely gone mad, and completely off the rails. But as the days went by, i just could not get this event, out of my head, it was like a nagging voice inside of me, saying you have got to do this, this is part of your life's journey, you must find the courage to do this. So eventually i found my inner courage to ring the number, that was displayed on the website. When the phone was eventually answered, it turned out to be a nice lady who only worked for the spiritual medium, making bookings, and appointments for her. I felt so nervous, and stupid at the time, but i briefly explained to her, how the sign on the back of car window, seemed to stand out to me, and almost illuminate to me in some way. I reluctantly told her, in a shy sort of way, about my new direction in life, explaining briefly to her, about some of the new, and strange events that had recently taken place within my life. I also explained to her further, that i was quite a shy person, and i also felt embarrassed, explaining these many new events to her, that had taken place in my life of late. I explained that i didn't really know why i was ringing her, but i felt inside, that i needed to do so. I was quite relieved to say the least, by her reply, she said she totally understood everything, that was happening to me, she also said that the spiritual medium, may have an important message, or direction for me to follow, in my life's journey. These words seemed to give me a new sense of inner relief, i also got a new feeling of strength, for overcoming my internal fear, of what people may think of me, for taking these new avenues in my life. I then, with great enthusiasm booked a appointment immediately to see the spiritual medium. My appointment was made for two days later, and it was going to take place at the spiritual mediums house. Then with a another set of strange circumstances, and the part i still find unbelievable, the spiritual medium only lived less than a five minute walk away from where i had worked all of my life. The next few days seemed to pass very quickly, and i will be honest with you, i was getting very nervous about my appointment with the spiritual medium. I think it was just the feeling of not knowing what to expect from the meeting with the her. I am sorry to say, that i didn't even mention this meeting, that i had arrange with anyone, especially my family members, or even my friends. I didn't know how they would react, or if they would even understand why i needed to see this person. My inner feelings at this time, was telling me to keep this meeting with the spiritual medium to myself, and maybe it would be possible to tell my family, and friends at some later date in my life's journey. I told my family that i was going to the local gym, for a workout, this part was quite tough for me, i hated the thought of not telling the truth to my family, and i didn't like myself for it at all. One hour before i was supposed to go to the planned appointment with the spiritual medium, i started to feel quite panicky, i was even getting butterflies in my stomach, i hadn't felt like this since going on my first date with a girl at school. I just didn't know what she would say, to these many new, and strange occurrences, that was taking place in my life. I tried to plan what i would say, and also what i wanted to ask her, but when the time eventually came for me to go, my mind went totally blank. When i eventually pulled in to the street where she lived, i recognized the area immediately. My garage only being five minutes away, i had towed in many cars from this area over the years. I eventually parked my car on the other side of the road, opposite the spiritual mediums house. Has i walked over to her house, my heart was beating faster, and faster, the palms of my hands were sweating heavily, i was even starting to shake as i approached the spiritual mediums door. At first i give the door a half hearted knock, my second knock seemed much louder. The spiritual medium then answered the door to me, i said hello, my name is Philip, i have an appointment to see you. As she replied to me, i got an immediate sense of calm, that seem to take over my whole body. I immediately got the same feeling you get, when you have known a person all your life, i seemed to feel totally at ease in her presence. I also knew that i had never met her before, but the feeling was there none the less. I introduced myself again, and sat down on the couch just opposite her. I started off, by telling her how i had seen the sign on the back of her car window, and how it seemed to glow to me. The spiritual medium thought that she may have a message for me, or she may be able to give me a direction for me to follow in my life's journey. I also explained how i had come across the law of attraction, she also seemed to have a knowledge about the law of attraction, but i felt the medium was more interested in the spiritual side of human life. I also explained to her, that i had also been investigating other areas of human life. Even though i wanted to mention, the many new incidents, that had recently taken place in my life, including the dove, and feathers that i had been finding everywhere, i couldn't seem to bring myself to mention them at this point. I was still not sure why i was really there, or what i really wanted to get from the meeting with her, but i had a inner feeling of calmness, in her presence. Then i seemed to want to tell her, that i had been reading many new books, and this was a new interest in life for me. I explained that, until recently i had never liked reading at all, and i was also never interested in books in general. I also explained to her that through a recent book, that i had read, i had learned to see the human aura field, she seemed quite surprised with that, and told me it was a good sign, that i could see the human energy field. The spiritual medium, then ask me to pick a card, from the deck that she was holding in her hands, i am not quite sure now, what the card exactly was, but she said to me, i had the energy of a healer, of some kind, and this may be a direction for me to take in my life's journey. The spiritual medium also seemed to pick up on me mentioning books to her, and she left the room and brought back about three books, i didn't even realize at the time, that i kept on mentioning books to her, but she seemed to pick up on this fact straight away, maybe it was my nerves, i am not quite sure. It didn't seem to matter anyway, she seemed to be able to pick up on everything straight away. She then handed me the three books for me to read, she said that she had not even read them herself, but she felt that she was supposed to give them to me anyway. I then assured her, that i would return them when i had read them all, but she seemed to act as though she didn't want them returning. She then returned to her feeling of me having the energy of a healer of some kind, i have got to be honest here, this was the first time i had heard anything like this, and it went straight over my head completely, how could i be a healer, i don't know the first thing about healing anybody. Even though i seemed to put this to the back of my mind, i had great respect for this spiritual medium, she seemed to have a great presence about her, i could also feel her strong energy inside the room, just being in the same room with her, was quite intoxicating. In my mind i was thinking, was this the message i needed to get about being a healer, or did the books contain the information i needed, to carry on with my life's journey. We both seemed to sit there, for a while not saying much, but i felt she was trying to read me, in some way, she then told me a bit about herself, and also her family. We then continued to chat for another ten minutes or so, i then felt its was time for me to go, i also think the spiritual medium, also felt that she had given me all of the information that she could at this point in time. She knew, that she had set me sail, on a new course in my life's journey so far. She also refused to accept any money from me, i am not quite sure why she didn't want to take payment, but i am truly grateful with all my heart, for the advice, and also the help that she as given me, on my life's journey, i truly wish her all the best in her future life, thank you!!!. One of the three books which the spiritual medium gave me that day, as completely change my outlook on the world of spirituality, god, and angels etc. The book was, Ask your Guides, by Sonia Chonquette. After reading this truly life changing book completely in just two short nights, i then immediately began realize, that the dove that turned up on my driveway, out of the blue, and also within a short space of time after jakes death, was the sign, that i had been asking, and waiting for. I believe this was the way, that Jake was letting me know that he was ok, and also doing just fine where he was, in his new home. I knew inside at the time, that this dove had a message of some kind for me, but until i read this amazing, and truly enlightening book, i feel that i was totally obliviously to this fact. After reading the important information contained within the pages of this valuable book, i seemed to get a instant relief, from all of the emotional pain, that i was still feeling at the time, from the great emotional loss of my best friend in life. I still felt inside myself, the great gap that Jake had left within me, and my families lives, but now i knew he was ok, the sadness of his death, just melted away. It was as though he was still here with us, and he had never truly left us at all. I now believe me visiting the spiritual medium, from talking with spirits was a way of me getting the book, to find out these valuable piece's of different information, so i could fill in the missing pieces of the jigsaw, so to speak. It all seemed to click into place, just when i needed it the most, to ease my great sense of loss, and also worry regarding Jake. I now know, that it was the fact of not knowing if Jake was ok, that seemed to cause me the most pain, after is death. When this one question was answered for me, in this truly amazing way, i believe i truly began to move on, and finally let go of the upset, and anger surrounding Jakes death. When i had the meeting with the spiritual medium, she also recommend that i attend one of her courses, for developing skills in the field of mediumship. But again something inside myself, seemed to let me know that i had got all of the information, and help that i could from the spiritual medium. This information would help me progress further on my life's journey. I also think the spiritual medium knew this to, even before she ask me the question, but i think she felt obliged to ask me anyway. At this point i was then starting to realize that the universe, God which ever you want to call this truly magical, and mysterious power, had many different ways, and means to get these very important, and much needed message's across to all of us, in our daily lives here on this amazing planet. I now know, that the many feathers i was seeing every where i went just after Jakes death, was my guardian angels watching over me, in a time of great need. The feathers was just a sign to me, to let me know i wasn't alone, and i am never truly alone in this life. Just this one thought gave my whole being, sensations of warmth, and true happiness. I now believe we all have guardian angles to watch over us, in our earthly domain, but we only tend to really see, and feel them, if we truly ask for their intervention in our daily lives here on earth. I have now come to a new understanding, that a great loss, or maybe a very traumatic event in our live's, will sometimes bring us to the point of new beginnings in our lives. These new beginnings may send us on a quest, for the true meaning of our lives here on this planet. Sometimes these very sad, and upsetting episodes in our lives, can be the key, to the door of our true path in this life, eventually leading us to true happiness in this life time. I feel sometimes we have to look past, the initial upset, and also fear, and even anger of these events in our lives, and begin to look at them, for the messages, and lesson's that they may contain regarding our future life. The answers we are looking for at these very difficult times in our lives, are probably staring us right in the face, we just have to open our hearts, and minds to see them. Some people may think this is strange and silly, and at first i did. But i couldn't put a rational explanation to the things that was continuing to happen all around me. I just felt that everything what was happening to me, felt so right inside of me. I knew that i was on journey, that i needed, and also wanted to embark on, i also knew that there was definitely no going backwards on this journey, the only way is to go forward. At this point of my own life's journey, i now feel a definite closeness to what many people on this planet refer to as God. What ever this mysterious entity or force maybe, i know feel him, or her more closer than ever before, affecting ever area of my daily life, and also my every thought, Thank you God.

CHAPTER 8

Discovering A New world

At this point in my life's journey, i carried on with my new passion for reading, with an even greater thirst, and quest for a greater understanding, and knowledge about these many new subjects, that were starting to take over every area of my daily life. One of these new books, that entered into my life, was by and amazing author called Doreen Virtue Phd. This book again seemed to cross my path, in another mysterious set of circumstances, it was called, Signs from Above. There was also another book title which, i again read with great excitement, and expectation, it was The Secret of Synchronicity, By Trish Macgregor, and Rob Macgregor. These two books are both truly amazing in their own right, they will begin to change your complete outlook on life, as you understand it now. These two enlightening books, have opened me up, to a new exciting, and magical world, that was once, completely invisible to me. These two special books, made me feel happy, and young inside again, they began to fill me with feelings of new discovery, and excitement about life. I felt like i was embarking on a magical quest of new discoveries, with feelings of excitement inside myself, which i had not felt, since i was a young child, just starting to discover, the strange new world that was all around me. Even though i have the beautiful, and wonderful gift of sight, i now feel i have been walking through most of my life totally blind. I mean this is the best possible way, its seems i have not been using this precious gift of sight at all. I feel like i have been in a state of sleep of some kind, totally oblivious to many parts of this astonishing life, that i have lived, for more than thirty nine years. I also feel that i am not the only one, on this planet, who is walking around in what i now call, a semi sleep like state of mind. I believe that it takes something dramatic, or even catastrophic to wake us up from this semi sleep like state of mind. But once this does happen in your life, its like waking up into a new and hidden world, that you never knew existed before this point. I believe once this process is set into motion, there is no going back to the semi sleep like state of mind, that you were once in. Once your eyes are truly open, and you have caught a glimpse of this magical, and hidden world, it is impossible to close them again. Even though it may be a rough ride at first, the light will eventually begin to shine through in every area of your daily life. I now feel at this point in time, we are all starting to awaken from our sleep like state's of being. Once we take a glimpse, into this hidden, and magical world, it as a profound effect on our entire being, it begins to open up our mind's to new possibilities of our true life purpose, hear on this planet now, giving us a true understanding of who we really are, here in this vast, and wonderful universe. The excitement at this moment in my life, is immeasurable, i have begun to fully awaken from my sleep like state of mind. I have begun to understand, that i have only ever seen my life, form a very narrow perspective indeed. My new zest, and quest for life, as felt quite daunting at certain points along my life's journey, i seemed to want to learn everything right away, trying to learn every little bit of new information that i came across. But i found, with patients everything begins to fall into place, you just have to give it some time, your life will start to be divinely guided in every way, you will begin to be awakened to the new, and magical realms of the invisible. I also feel that it's never to late to find your true path in this life, and start to discover the true treasures, that await you on your life's journey this time around. I now strongly feel that i was guided to the two books, which i mentioned earlier in this chapter, i also feel i was guided to them, just at the right time in my life's journey. Both these special books seemed to appear in my life, just when i needed the information most. I cannot emphasize strongly enough, the impact that both of these books, have had on my life, i feel that they have opened up, a new area contained within my heart, and began the process of true enlightenment in my life. That said, i would therefore strongly recommend, the reading of these two special, and also life changing books, when you find, that you are guided to them, on your own life's journey. Some people may say, that me recommending these powerful books to you now, would not be the same as being divinely guided to them. But i feel if your reading my words now at this point, you have already been divinely guided to them through the words contained in the pages of this book. This is how i have discovered the many books titles, on my own life's journey so far. I felt that i was also guided to many other books, from recommendation contained within the pages of the books, that i was reading at the time. I also feel now at this point, you can never predict, where the guidance will come from, but come it will, you just need to have the faith, that it will eventually come. What these two truly revolutionary books are basically saying to all of us, is that we are all getting pointers, and signs, every where in our daily lives, i literally mean we are being given divine guidance, and help, in every area of our human existence, here on this planet. We are all being watched over by this mysterious, and unseen force, which seems to fill all of what we call the empty space around us. At some point we all tend to ignore these many pointers, and guidance in our daily lives, but sometimes the consequences of this, can be disastrous to say the least. It seems that every second, and every minute, of every day of our lives in this physical realm, we are all being divinely guided in every single way. At first this mysterious force begins to show its self, with little nudges in every area of our your life, it try's to push us along our chosen tasks, or path in this life time, encouraging us to take, or follow a certain direction, along our true life's purpose. I also know from my own personal experience, that when we refuse to see, or decide to turn away from these many messages, and signs, trying to shy away from our true life purpose here on planet earth, life begins to become a struggle, in every sense of the word. Many things start to go wrong in all areas of our lives, ranging from our family lives, right down to our work careers, and money, eventually even our health begins to suffer. If we then still choose to ignore and fight, these divine messages, and pointers to our true life's path, life can become extremely miserable, and depressing. I don't believe, for a minute, that this great mysterious power, which i feel surrounds everything we see, and also cannot see, as anything to do with trying to harm us in any way. What i do believe is that we all arrive in this physical body, with a life purpose, a mission in this life. The hurt, and the struggle, i believe only comes from within ourselves, with our constant daily fight with our earthly lives, which we have chosen this time around. This divine source, which is a part of all of us, is only trying to put us back on track, to discovering our true life's path, which in turn, will lead us to true happiness in our earthly lives this time around. I believe it already knows what our chosen path is, and it is constantly trying to steer us onto this path, and lead us back to true happiness in this life time. I feel somewhere along human existence, we have lost our ability to pick up on these daily communications from our true source. There as been a sort of communication breakdown, in the divine connection within ourselves. I feel that when we begin to awaken from this sleeping state of mind, we call reality, the communication with the divine seems to start again, opening up a new channel of communication to our true divine source of inner being. This connection is within all of us, but i feel that most of us have lost it, somewhere along our human evolutionary path here on this planet. This as in turn, brought us into a state of disconnection from who we truly are, i think we all feel this disconnection deep down inside our selves, giving us this empty feeling deep within our ourselves. I believe this disconnection can be described in many ways, from the feeling of deep depression, to a feeling of being unfulfilled in our lives. I also believe this disconnection if continued, can in time develop into what we call physical illnesses within our bodies, and also our minds. I know this, with a sense of certainty, that as you read the words in the pages of this book, they will begin to resonate inside of you, bringing you, to a sense of inner knowing, that there is much more to you, than you could of ever imagined, beyond your wildest dreams. Putting an end, to the illusion that we are just physical beings here in this vast universe. We truly are, eternal beings in every way, i also feel this is one of life's greatest secret's, i truly believe this with all my heart. Just this one discovery of our external existence, is enough to fill my heart with love, and true happiness, ending my search for one of the biggest question's i have been asking myself, from the day, i was born into this world. The amazing feeling of knowing these truths, will begin to open up, many new doorways in every area of your life, and consciousness. The great physical illusion of our daily lives, and daily problems, including our many routines, will all start to show themselves for what they truly are, just a construct of our egotistic minds. That for so long, we have been unable to get past, but this lifting of the veil, will seem like a breath of new fresh air, that will begin blow straight through every part of your body, and mind. You will begin to see that we are not at all separate from each other, but the total opposite is true, we are all connected through a wider spiritual consciousness. You will begin to see that our daily lives are divinely guided in every single way, you will also begin to open up, to the many messages, that you have been receiving in your every day life, from the very beginning of your existence. These message's truly hold the key to our happiness in this life time, and the more we begin to use this guidance in our every day life, the more love, and happiness will begin to pour into to it. I know this from my own personal experience, this powerful guidance literally as the power to change your life in ways you could only dream of. Once we truly begin to look for this divine messaging system, and truly begin to open our hearts and mind's to it, you will begin to see them everywhere you look, little pointers, nudges, and guidance in every part of your life. I started to pick up on many new things, i would of never noticed before, it was like i was being introduced to a totally new world. Many things around me in nature, animals, trees's, weather, clouds etc, all seemed to be giving me, this new guidance in my daily life. I now know, that they have always been there guiding me, but i was just shut off from them, not being able to understand them in my life. Before what i now call my awakening, i would have never given any of these many message's, pointers, and signs, a second thought. But now i know one hundred percent, and with all my heart, that we are all being guided by this invisible powerful force, if we like i, or not, it is a fact of our lives, as human beings here in this vast, seen, and unseen universe. I believe at this point in time, this very important information is still only understood, and practiced, by a very small percentage of this planet. But at last, there are very encouraging signs, that we as human beings, are starting to awaken, and discover this great, and powerful knowledge. It is, at last starting to spread across all areas of the planet, bringing new, and powerful changes to in all areas of humanity. Happiness, love, abundance, and peace, is being brought back into the lives of millions, around our amazing planet. I believe when you start to begin your own life's journey, you will also start to notice, just silly little things at first, like when your having a bad day, or nothing seems to going your way. Then all of sudden, you will be stopped in your track's, by finding a simple penny on the floor, or maybe a feather just seems to appear from no where. This simple penny, or feather makes you stop and think, just for a second, or you may even pick it up, and just for that second it pulls your attention away from your daily worries, and stresses of this modern daily life. But with our hectic life styles of today, we just don't see these as important message's in our lives, telling us to stop what were doing, and just take a breath, and try to reflect on the current situation, of what were are doing to ourselves at that moment in time. We tend just to carry on, and ignore these important messages, and move on with our day to day lives, with all of their problems, and never ending drama's. We loose the meanings of these many pointers, and message's, without even realizing what they were, and the treasure's that they may have held for us in our lives. I think if we all give ourselves a chance, and just look around in our daily life routines, i know we will all begin to see the great truth's, of this truly magical life, here on earth.

CHAPTER 9

Numerology

I t was a couple of weeks later, when i again, seemed to be guided to a new, and fascinating book, on the subject of numerology. After reading this enlightening new book, a number of times, i really had the chance to learn all of the new, and important information that was contained within its pages. I felt so excited about this new information that i had discovered. I began to feel that i had discovered another part of this hidden world, within our own world. I felt another doorway, had just been opened again for me, by the pages of this truly illuminating book about the ancient art of numerology. This was the first time, i had heard of numerology, and from the very first pages, i was completely blown away, by how powerful this information truly was. I had a inner feeling, that this information was meant to be shared with the world, it seemed far to important, to be known, by only a few. The very second i started to fully understand this powerful information, i had an immediate urge inside myself, it was like a inner knowing, that i must do my very best to share this important information with as many people as possible. This was a whole new way of looking at numbers, i have got to be honest, i was never a great fan of maths, or any sort of number related subjects. At school, i found that i was never particularly interested in numbers or anything related to them, but numerology was definitely a different way, of looking at numbers. After reading my first book on the subject, over and over again, i began to see numbers in a totally new, and exciting light. I became totally fascinated with this new world of numerology, i also started to download numerology apps to my iPhone, using them to discover more, and more about this fascinating, and new subject in my life. I also began to check out many different sites on the internet, the many sites that i came across held vast amounts of truly amazing, and new information regarding this truly life changing subject. I started to find out, about my birth number, my soul number, and also my life's path number. I then began to fully awaken, and truly realize the true importance, that these three numbers, had in my life. With Just a little research, and study, i found out to my complete astonishment, and without me even realizing it, my birth number, my soul number, and my life's path number, have followed me all the way through my entire life. From the very day i was born, right up till my present day life. When i began to look back through my life, my previous house's, contained these numbers in their addresses. The many car registration i had owned through my life, contained these numbers, my best friends had these numbers in their name conversions. The many places i liked to visit contained these numbers in their letter conversions to. Even the pin numbers to my credit cards contained these numbers, it was really freaky at first, it just seemed like it could be a story from the movies. I then realized that these number connections were everywhere i looked, right down to the jobs i had work in, and even the places where i still worked today. It seemed every part of my life contained these special numbers in some way, this discovery then sent me on a new quest to find the meaning's, and also the significance that these three special number's may hold in my life. I needed to find out every bit of information i could regarding these three numbers, and what they meant for me on my life's path this time around. Once you discover your own numerology numbers, with regard to your own life, you will then begin to notice, that they play apart in every area of your own life, here on this planet. The numbers two, nine, and three are my special numbers, i would see two, and nine every single morning, illuminated on a bus number display board, on my drive to work. Until this point i had never noticed this before, i would also see the same numbers on lamp post's, digital clocks etc, these numbers really began to stand out to me. At this point, they again seemed to have a glowing effect around them, this strange effect seemed to happen every single time i laid my eyes on them. The most important thing i began to discover, was the meaning of numbers in my life. As part of my daily job, i would perform many road test of cars through my working day, it seemed like every time i would test a car, the same bus would be passing my works, at the exact same time, when i would be testing a vehicle. The bus had the numbers two, and nine on it's display board, this seemed to give me butterflies in my stomach ever time it would happen. There were also the words collins green written next to the numbers, and even these words stood out to me at that this point in time. The words seemed to have no meaning to my life, at this point of my life's journey, but i would later find out their true meaning for me, at a later date. At this point i would truly urge every body reading this book now, to try numerology out for yourselves, i know with all my heart, it will change the way you look at your life forever. This may seem quite far fetched to some people, but please put your skepticism aside for thirty minutes, and try it out for yourself. There are many internet sites, which are willing to work out your special numerology numbers for you in only a few minutes, and its free. The internet site's, will also tell you, your number meanings, giving you a glimpse into this mysterious hidden world. Many people may say you are only seeing these numbers now, because you are looking for them, but once you experience this for yourself, you will know its a different feeling entirely. You don't just see the numbers, you also begin to feel them, they give you a sense of inner knowing, a message, or meaning to your life. Don't waste any more time do it now, its totally free, and only takes minutes to do, all you need is your full name, and date of birth. The only part i didn't fully understand was why i was finding out this special information, at this point in my life's journey, why didn't i find this important information much earlier in my life, so i could of used it, to direct my life in better ways. I now feel inside that this important information, only begins to arrive when we are truly ready to accept it into our lives, and we are also able to act on it, for the better good of mankind as a whole. But i feel, if you are reading this book now, at this point in time, then you to are also ready, to receive this valuable life changing information. I began to get a feeling inside, that i was led to numerology because it contained a very important message for the direction i should take in my life's path so far. When i looked, deeper and closer into the meaning of my three personal numbers, which were tied to my destiny in life, it all began to make perfect sense, and also have great meaning to my life. The information contained within these numbers described my personality perfectly, right down to the very last detail. At first i thought, no thats not me at all, thats wrong, but when i truly searched my inner deeper feelings, i knew it was all true. The vast wealth of information contained within these three little numbers, was truly astonishing to me. I have listed, a very brief description about their meanings for the purpose of this book, which are as follows. My birth number was nine, my destiny number was two, and my soul number was three. Even though, there were slightly different variations in their descriptions, from the many books, that i had already read on numerology, and also the many internet sites, that i had discovered. They all seemed to be, in a general agreement, on their meanings, i was a generous large hearted person, caring and romantic, but i already knew this, i was born on valentines day. I was definitely a family person, cared for humanity at large, and i was probably drawn towards a career in the arts, and would possibly be successful. There was also information in the numbers that seemed to say, i may have healing abilities of some kind, and a life's path of some sort of healer. This was the second time, i had come across this information regarding healing, but this time it seemed to have a greater meaning to me, and it gave me goose bumps all over my body. This is also where i found my new urge to start writing, i feel deep down that i have always wanted to write since my early childhood. I have always had wild, and exotic dreams, and always thought about putting these dreams to good use. But something inside myself always stop me from doing it, i was never really sure why. I will still continue to research this fascinating subject of numerology, but i feel that numerology as already given me the most important message's, and pointers in my life's journey so far, and i fully intend to use them with all my heart. I cannot recommended enough to anybody who is trying to find their way in life, or a meaning to their life, to buy a book on numerology, or go to one of the many numerology sites on the internet, to find out your own numerology information. You might be very surprised, and thrilled to what you will find out about your true self, or even what you don't know about yourself. Everything i have read regarding my own numbers rung totally true in every area, and detail of my life. I hope with all my heart that, your special numerology numbers, open's many new doors way's in your path of life.

CHAPTER 10

Questions

After hearing the word healing again, and the possibility of having a life path, which may include the gift of writing, i immediately started to look at both of these new subjects in my life, with a totally different out look. I also began to think thoughts, along the line's, of one of these subjects being a new possible career option for me, in the not to distant future. At that moment, i also began to open up my heart to the very real possibility that this is what i have always wanted in my life, maybe these new career's are part of my true life's path, here on this planet, this time around. I began to get a sense of inner peace from the thoughts of becoming a healer, and also a possible writer. I had this strange feeling inside myself, that i had always knew this, from the very beginning of my birth in to this world, but for some strange, and unknown reason, i had kept these desires, and feelings hidden deep within myself, locked away, and unable to reach them. I am still not sure why these many new feeling's, have only just surfaced into my awareness, but i feel that until this point in my life, i would have not been ready to accept any of these new understandings about my life, and i would of probably, veered away from them in my early life, sending me on a path of total chaos, and misdirection. I know somewhere inside of me, i feel that i have always wanted to heal people in some way, i would even goes a far as saying, that at this point in my life's journey, my feelings of healing are so strong, that in fact they are feelings of needing to heal, rather than wanting to heal. Maybe this is the true key to healing my own life, i started to sense, and also feel that the more i started to move towards these new paths in my life, the more my life seem to flow, with much less resistance, and lots more happiness in all area's of my entire life. With this new sense of peace in my life, i also started to get a uncontrollable urge to write down, what i was going through on my life's journey, covering these last year's or so of my life. At first i tried to ignore these urges, and many pointers, my ego would start to kick in, i started to feel inner fear, and tell myself, you can't be a healer you don't know the first thing about healing people, or you definitely couldn't be a writer, you can hardly put a sentence together. This was made worse by the fact, i was never great at putting pen to paper, even in my early school years, my teachers at school could never read my scruffy handwriting, and they would always complain about my bad punctuation, and poor use of the english language. I continued to tell myself that i couldn't possibly write a book, or heal anybody, i was trying my hardest to convince myself, and find any reason i could, not explore these new paths in my life. But the more i tried to fight these urges to write, and to follow a healing path, the stronger the urges, and nudges seemed to get. Eventually i got to a stage, where the urges were so strong, i could no longer ignore them. It was starting to effect me physically, and mentally, i began to feel totally drained, right down to my inner core, and existence. At that very moment, when i decided to go with my inner guidance, instead of against it, i felt a waterfall of energy, enter my whole being. This new energy seemed to cleanse me, right down to my inner soul. The feeling of my body, and mind being drained seemed to totally leave me, and a surge of enthusiasm and creativity, seemed to enter my entire body. I then, at that point started to put my fingers to my computer keyboard, and not pen to paper, which seemed the perfect option for me, what with spell check, and the really neat fonts on my mac, it felt so right for me. This was the start of my love affair, with writing, and also the start of my first book, **Discovering Many of Life's Mysteries, and Secrets's On My Own Life's Journey So Far.** I think i have always had something inside of me, a feeling of trying to express myself in some way, but i was never quite sure how to do it. With writing, i now think i may have found that way to express myself perfectly. I can still remember as a child, having very strange dreams of outer space, and many other far out wild dreams that i mentioned in earlier chapters. Many mornings when i awoke from my deep exploring sleep, as a young child, i always said to myself, i could make a movie, or write a book about these wild, and strange dreams someday. But sadly, i never seemed to have the right motivation, until now. My mind again started to fill with many more questions, to these many new life changing experiences, that i now seemed to be having now on a daily basis. I needed to find the answers to this ever expanding list of many different questions, that i was getting on a daily basis. At this point in my life's journey, i started to practice the art of meditation, on a daily basis. Many of the books that i had already read on my life's journey so far, expressed the true importance of daily meditation in life, and nearly all of the authors who had written the books, practiced this in their own daily life routines. I will be honest at first, i found it so hard to even relax in any way, my body seemed stiff, to the extent of saying it was in a tormented, and twisted state of being. I feel this was caused from the many years of constant stress, anger, and deep frustration with my life. The first part of meditation, i learnt, was the art of getting your mind into the silence. Many of books i have read, refer to this as a quieting of the inner mind, from the daily chaos of the physical realm, which we all inhabit, here on this planet. Even though at first, it felt like a struggle, i again felt something inside of me, and inner feeling that it was something i needed, and must do for myself, on my life's journey so far. I knew inside, that i was again being guided towards using meditation in my daily life routine, it just felt like it was the next step in stone in my life's journey. It all seemed to follow a familiar pattern of guidance, that i had already seen for myself, on many occasions previously. I would start to see signs about meditation everywhere i looked, from my computer emails, television, even adverts on the back of a buses, seemed to drum home the subject of meditation. The many different pointers, and message's i felt i was getting, again seemed to have a sort of glow, or shine to them. They totally stood out to me, in a way that was totally unmistakable, and also unmissable. It was exactly the same phenomena, that i had experienced with the sign on the back of the mediums car, which i had visited, many months before, in my life's journey. Again the more i ignored these pointers, thinking meditation just wasn't for me, the more intense, and unavoidable the messages became. I eventually found the urges, and many pointers, to strong to ignore any longer. I found myself giving into these constant nudges, and started to practice the art of meditation on a daily basis. After only a few weeks of practicing the ancient, and sacred art of meditation, and learning, and trying different variations, and styles of meditation, the effect of my life was truly amazing. I feel that within only a couple of weeks, of using this sacred art of meditation, my consciousness as gone through a monumental shift in its awareness, of who we true truly are. This new feeling inside of me, led me into a dramatic shift, of not wanting to be without meditation in my daily life experience. I was truly shocked at first, by these very strong feelings, and emotions, about meditation. It felt like meditation was a sort of key to my inner knowing, and inner soul, and it felt like i had just turned the lock. It just felt like, i had opened up to another level of consciousness. In the weeks that followed, i just couldn't seem get enough of it, meditation that is. I began to look forward to my meditation sessions, it was a sort of anticipation. I felt like i was getting the answers to my many questions, when i was in this trance's like state of mind. It seemed to give my whole body, a great sense of inner peace, and wellness, it was almost like having my body recharged after a hard day's work. My physical health also began to improve, in many different ways. My energy levels began to soar to amazing new heights. Meditation also seemed to act as a pain killer, but it turned out to be much more than that for me. When in deep meditation, or the silence which ever you want to call it, i seemed to start getting flashes of thought's, answers to the many questions i had been asking myself for many months. A lot of the time, i didn't even know i was asking some of these questions, its quite hard to explain until you have tried it for yourself, which i defiantly recommend you do, on a regular basis, daily if possible. I started off my meditation, by doing twenty minutes a day, and gradually working up to thirty minutes, sometimes, i would even go into a trance like state of mind, for an hour or so. I quickly found out, that when you are doing your meditation, you need to be alone for that period of time, and some where you will not be disturbed. I found that being in a peaceful environment greatly enhanced the power, and also the feeling of the meditation, which in turn give my body immeasurable benefits. Later I started to learn you can even meditate when your walking alone, or gardening alone, anything where your alone, and you have the time to relax, and go inward, into the silence, and quite your outer thoughts, is a kind of meditation. I cannot begin to explain the benefits of meditation, it as totally de-stressed my body, and when you totally quite your mind, and start to relax your body in this way, its a feeling of utter pleasure, and total bliss. My body's health improved dramatically, from the peaceful, and relaxing affects of doing my daily meditation. Meditation started to actually change the way i looked and felt about my self. I started to glow from the inside out, i began to look much younger in every way. The people many different around me, in my daily, also began to notice it to. I was getting amazing comments off my friends, and family, about how good, and fresh i looked. My garage customers at work, started to say you look bright, and fresh today, you seem to get younger every time we bring our car in, whats your secret. I myself started to notice these many changes within me, my energy levels began to far exceeded the levels prior to doing the meditations, in my life. I then knew from that point on, i had discovered a very special secret in the art of meditation. This ancient, and sacred art of meditation, can truly add years, of vigor to your life. This discovery really does mean that you really don't need, all of the anti aging products on the markets these day's, the best anti aging cure, and health enhancing product, is meditation by far. I wanted to tell everybody about this amazing new part to my life, and let them all know about these amazing health benefits from meditation. My aching back of many years, which has caused me great discomfort and pain, over the many years of my life, was also starting to ease, and heal itself. Up and till this point in my life, i had tried many different things over the years to help with my back problems, but to date i had only limited, to no success with all of them. And here i was, after only a few months into meditation, with what i can only call the miracles, and health cures of deep meditation, Thank you.

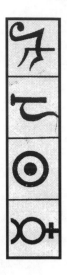

CHAPTER 11

My health

At this point in my life's journey, i now know that most of my health problems in life, have originated from my very stressful work environment. Working in a family run business is no easy task, which i am sure many reader's of this book, who work in a family run business, will agree and fully understand. I know that working in a family business, also brings with it many advantages, but it also brings, many unwanted disadvantages, which i now know, and also feel was the cause of my many health problems, in my life to date. I now realize that my personal life, and also my work life, was totally out of balance, and because of this, my health was suffering greatly. With this new understanding about my health problems, being linked with my stressful work environment, i began to change, and turn this around immediately. The first signs of doing this, was the great improvement in my back problems. I started to realize that my back was getting gradually better by the day, i also noticed that i was not getting stressed out, as easy as i did before. I seemed to be dealing with stressful situations at work, and at home in a much better way, than i had done perviously in my life. Before this point in my life, the slightest little things, may have sent me into a angry, and stressful rage. But now i just seemed to be in better control of my daily life, including my work life, which made them both a lot more enjoyable. This greatly enhanced all areas of my life, i was beginning to see a universal improvement everywhere. I began to understand, that you can either attract negative situations in your life, which in turn can also affect your bodies physical, and mental health, or your can attract positive situations in your life, which will greatly enhance your physical, and mental health, the choice really is your own. We have all been there when something starts to go wrong at work, or at home, you start stressing, shouting arguing with family, and work colleges, then the day just seems to go from bad to worse. You can literally feel the bad vibrations building from within yourself, starting to snowball into something much worse. Waiting for disaster, to appear just around the next corner, with a total ignorance to what damage, we are also doing to our selfs, physically, and also mentally. What i have eventually realized, and believe me this as taken me a half a life time to fully understand this, when something does go actually wrong in your life, and as we all know, it definitely will at some point. Even though what i am about say, is not a easy thing to do, and its much, much easier in life, just to flip out, and totally loose control of yourself. Starting to blame every body else around you, for the negative situation, you may find yourself in, at that point in time. Instead of this negative option, just stand back for a minute, take a deep breath. Take a real deep look at the situation again, re-evaluate it for what it really is, and i guarantee you, you will find that most of the time, your own inner feelings, and thoughts are the ones that are really betraying you, causing you all the upset, pain, and stress at that very moment. Then the really serious, and big problem you think you may have had, is only something really stupid, and not really worth all of the upset, and anger, it as created within yourself. But we all work ourselves into such a emotional frenzy sometimes, it just seems to blind our common sense. You would sometimes think many of these silly little dramas, that we play out with each other in our daily lives, was a life threatening moment, by our vast over reaction's to many of them. I feel that we just need to see past that initial flash point, and say to ourselves from within, is this situation really that bad, how can i turn this into a positive situation, and escape this potential upset. I feel that our own inner analysis, at these times is the key to dealing with them, when you just step back and look from a different view point, any negative situation, can be turned into a positive one. Please just give this a try for yourself, and you will be able to transform your life in ways that you could only dream of. I am not saying this will be easy, in fact it is one of the most difficult things i have ever needed do in my life, and believe me, it will not happen over night. There will be many occasions, when you will not be able to control your strong inner emotions, and things will at certain times, go dramatically wrong in a big way. But i feel that these flash points, can also be a great lesson's, bringing to our attention again, the silliness of our inner reactions to some of life's most trivial problems. You will began to keep watch on your emotions, ever vigilant of these dangerous, and unhealthy actions. I believe, if we just start to flip the balance in our behavior patterns, and start to shift, and turn away from the negative situations, and emotions, and start to replace them with the more positive situations, and feeling's, you will begin to change your life for the better in every way. You alone have the God given power within you, to view, and also change, all of the supposed negative events, and situations in your daily life, and really begin to see them for what they really are. You can begin to change them, for what you really want them to be, removing these so called negative illusions, that plague, and fill many of our daily lives here on this wonderful planet, we call Earth. Begin to use your vast power, as a human being, to change all of your negative events in your life, into the positive events of your life. Start to use them to your own advantage, and don't give away your power to them. I promise you the effects on your general well being, and health will be nothing short of a miracle. I myself began to feel, i had control back in my life again, something i had not felt for such a long time. In fact till this point, i don't think i have ever felt in this much control of my life before. What i mean by this statement is, up until this point in my life, i feel as though my life, as been totally out of my control, but i now feel, that i am back at the wheel, steering the ship into much calmer, and clearer waters. I have got to stress again at this point, and be totally honest with you, this will be very hard for anybody attempting to take control of their life in this way, and it will not happen over night, and neither will it be plane sailing all the way. But once you do, once you tip that balance, the rewards will be truly amazing, changes will appear in every area of your life, from health, money, happiness, joy, and love. I feel i have rediscovered the most precious gift of all, the one we all seem to take for granted at sometime in our lives, good health. Once my health had started to return, only then did i realize the full extent of my health issues, which i had been living blind to, for so many years. In some way i had just seemed to have accepted all of them, as part of old age. The truth is, we can all live healthy lives, even into very old age, its only the emotional stresses, we put on our selves in our day to day lives, that will eventually turn themselves into physical, and mental illnesses.

CHAPTER 12

Healing, And The Human Aura

At this stage of my life's journey, i feel that i have started to heal my life, and also my body, i truly started to understand more, and more that we ourselves, are the greatest healer of our own bodies, here in this physical reality. It was again at this point of my life's Journey, where i again turned to my new trusted source of information, and knowledge, books. I felt i was again guided to many new books, on the subject of healing. I read every one of these new book's, with great enthusiasm, and also great speed. I really started to understand, and discover many new healing techniques. I also began to implement many of these new healing techniques on my own body, it seemed that i was discovering new healing techniques on a daily basis, from my many new, and wide ranging sources of information. With this new powerful knowledge of healing, i also discovered, and seemed to be be guided to the ancient art of yoga. I have always kept myself physically fit, when i had the time, and energy to do so. I would always participate, in many of the physical activities, at my local gym, with my family, and also my friends. But with yoga, this felt totally different for me, it seemed to re-energize my body, and also my mind in a totally different way. The effects on my body, and mind, was totally different from any of the other physical activities, that i had gotten used to, over the many years, that i had been training my physical body. This ancient art started to give my body, feelings of newness, and also youngness again. My body felt full of vibrant new energy, i seemed to be thinking much clearer, and straighter, than i had ever done before. My little aches, and pains started to vanish from all parts of my body. My tight muscles, which i had been putting up with, for many years, were starting to free themselves off, i felt truly amazing in every way. Weeks later i was in my upstairs bathroom, giving myself a good grooming in front of the mirror. This was a quite new experience for me, i was starting to notice a definite change, in my attitude towards my physical body. I have always looked after myself, but this was totally different, i really started to care for myself again. It was a feeling of falling in love with myself all over again, in a good way i mean, there was no ego, or arrogance involved here, just a pure respect for myself, down to the deepest core of my inner self. I began to notice, that i was taking special care of myself again, right down to the very smallest of details, i was pampering myself, like never before, and it felt great!!!. Anyway, back to what i was just trying to tell you, before i got myself side tracked. As i was grooming myself in front of the mirror, i seen something, just out of my peripheral vision, and it immediately caught my attention. I started to notice a whitey, blue thick luminous halo around the top of my head, and also around the tops of my shoulders, and arms. At first i only noticed it for a couple of seconds, then it seemed to vanish. I did mention this aura experience, briefly in the previous chapters, when i had my meeting with the spiritual medium, which was much earlier, in my life's journey. But this time, it was totally different. Before this point, i had only been seeing little glimpses of my own body aura, like a faded coloured mist. I had also noticed this mist around a few other people. But now this new, and more luminous effect, totally blown me away. When you first see this life changing event, you start thinking is there something wrong with my eyes. I started to think to myself, am i really seeing this, or is this, just my imagination. All sorts of questions, started to race around inside my mind. I stood there, looking at myself, for two or three minutes, and the more i looked, just out of my eyes focus, the stronger the luminous halo appeared around my head, and also my shoulders. As time went on, it even began to show down the side's of my whole body, the more i looked, the more it began to stay in my eyes focus, and also for much longer periods of time. I had read about this amazing phenomenon, much earlier in my life's journey, the book i read was by James Redfield, The Celestine Prophecy. But to be honest at that time, i just thought this was a fictional phenomenon, rather than actual fact. I thought my earlier experiences of the human aura field were amazing, but this new effect, was like seeing my actual life force energy, surrounding my entire body, it was totally mind blowing in every way. I knew now, at this very point, it was totally one hundred percent real in every way, and it definitely was not, a trick of my eyes. I knew i needed to find out more about this new, and magical phenomenon right away. I immediately started to research the subject further through the many internet sites, that seemed to cover this fascinating subject in greater detail. I also located a few new books on this special subject, but there only seemed to be a few books, that covered the subject of the human aura field. This time, the internet seemed to be, the far better source of information, regarding this new, and mysterious subject, in my life. The internet, give me the chance to study this mysterious phenomena in much greater detail. I came to understand that what i was seeing was definitely the human aura energy field. This gift, or ability which i like to call it, can begin to happen to people, when they are awakening spiritually. The true fact is, every human being on this planet, as the ability to see their aura field, but most of us, have forgotten how to see it, and also how to use it, to our own advantages. I now realize that at first, i was just catching glimpses of the aura field, through the misty colours, that i was seeing. But this time, in my bathroom looking into the mirror, with a bit of concentration involved, also with a totally white background, behind me, which i now know through my research efforts, makes it much easier to see the human aura field. With these many new understandings, that i was just discovering, i started to look at my self in the mirror, preferably in my top floor bathroom, where its was totally whited out. As i started to look at myself, over and over again, in my top floor bathroom mirror, the same lightish bluish ring, was now starting to extend about four, to five inches around my head, and also my shoulders. Its so hard to put into words here in this book, on how i actually felt, when i was seeing this aura energy field around myself. To say it was another life changing moment for me, is really a understatement. I was actually seeing myself for what i truly was, a spiritual, eternal being, encased in a physical body here on earth. Believe me, when you actually see this aura field for yourself, and with your own eyes, i think you will also have a hard time trying to describe, how you actually feel inside of your self, at that very moment. Its much, much harder, trying to describe it here, with only words, you just need to experience this magical moment for yourself. I guarantee you, just this one thing above any other will change your life, and also your outlook on human beings forever. Once you initially see your aura energy field, you just cannot stop looking at it. You will become fascinated by this newly discovered part of your self, that you have been blind to, and living without for so long. This new discovery about life, starts to fill your whole being with joy, and amazement. I felt i had discovered, one of life's enduring mysteries, the illusion that we are just a physical body, was truly and completely over for me that day. I had been introduced to a much larger, and magical world. In the days that followed, i think i was still in state of shock, in a nice way i mean, i wanted to shout it from the roof top's, tell all my family, what i had discovered, in this amazing secret. But i wasn't sure how to tell them, or if i should tell them at all, they may again think, that i had totally lost my mind this time. They had already seen some quite dramatic changes in me, over the past month's of my life, and i didn't want to push there understanding, of this new world, that i was discovering. But my excitement got the better of me, and i told my son Kyle. I am not sure, but he also said he could see it, but may be, he was just trying to be nice to me, i am still not sure. I now know from my research that all human beings, and animals on this planet, have the ability to see this aura energy field, that surrounds our bodies. I also know from my further research, that when we are born into this world, we are born with this ability, to see this energy field. This is why new born babies, tend to look just above peoples heads, because they are said to be looking, at the bright aura halo, which surrounds the persons head. But unfortunately, we all seem to loose this amazing sense, around three years of age. This is said to happen, because of our many earthly distractions, and our love of this material world, which surrounds us, and becomes more, and more real to us, the older we get. I do not fully understood the reason, why this ability as been given back to me, at this point in my life's journey. But i feel, truly grateful to be able to see, this amazing part of ourselves, that i have been blind to for so long. I also feel, most of humanity, as also forgotten about this truly amazing gift. Many of the worlds ancient cultures, thousands of years old, truly knew the importance of this hidden human sense. This amazing ability, was used in their daily lives for the diagnose's of health issues, emotional problems, and in many other area's, of there human lives. It seemed to be another turning point for me, and a sort of step up if you like. I seemed to feel more empowered, with this new sense, and ability that i had been gifted with, or i had been re-awakened to. For weeks, this new ability seem to take over me completely, i wanted to try and enhance it. I still couldn't really find any books regarding the subject, but the internet seemed to be a vast wealth of knowledge on this amazing subject, so i carried on my research there. With my new research, i also began to find out, that i wasn't the only one around our planet, who was re-discovering this lost ability. It seemed this was happening, all over our planet. There was definitely a shift, taking place in the human consciousness, as a whole. I had already read this in many of the books along my life's journey so far. But now i was seeing, and feeling it for my self. I felt inside, that this ability being re-discovered by so many people around the planet, was just the start, of a much bigger awakening to come. This was mind blowing, it was like the people of the planet was going through some sort of conscious shift, and starting to re-awaken to their true selves. It seemed a shift, of great magnitude in human evolution, was starting to take place, and begin to happen in our time, now on this planet. This was very exciting times for me, this again only seemed to clarify many of the things, i had read in the numerous books on my life's journey so far. Many of the worlds ancient cultures from around the globe, had also documented this change, many thousands of years before it would happen. They said that it would mark, a new era, in our understanding of who we really are, in this vast universe. They say seeing, is truly believing, and i hope my experience will drive you, to re-learn this amazing ability, and gift for your self, and begin your own awakening into a new era, of human evolution on this planet. The most easy way, to re-learn this ability, is to look into any mirror, preferably with a light background behind you, pure white is perfect for learning. As you stand there looking straight at your self, focus on the point between your eyes, or just above. With a little practice and patients, hopefully you will begin to see your own aura energy field, coming into your focus. At first you may only catch little glimpses of it, but practice makes perfect. I believe its like a muscle, and the more you begin to use it again, and remember its great power, which as always been within you, the easier it will become. I also believe it will change the way you see yourself forever. If this is the only thing you take from this book, then i have done you a great service, in your own life.

CHAPTER 13

Another Piece of The Puzzle

To me, it just seemed like i had found, a very large piece of this great jigsaw puzzle we call our lives here on this planet. From this point on, my amazing life's journey started to take on, a new sense of great excitement, anticipation, and mystery. I couldn't help but look further, and further into this new aura phenomena. I felt like child again, the excitement of finding something totally new, and magical within my life. These new feelings, began to fill me, with large amounts of energy, and a new quest, for living life to the full. I carried on watching, many more videos on the internet, just so i could clarify, the many questions, that were going around in my head. I wanted to be sure, that i was getting the best information i could, regarding these many new subject's in my life. To be honest at this point, there was a lot of people saying, they was able to see all sorts of colours around people, and other livings things. But i felt this was different for me, this wasn't really what i was seeing. I could still see, the faded misty colours, around different people, but by far the most prominent colour for me, was the light blue glowing mist, or aura which extended four to five inches around the body, with what i call a translucent glow, around the edges. The faded misty colours, that i could also see, extended much further away from the body, they appeared in all different colours, even grayish colours. The bluish field, i was seeing, was closet to the body, and it really started to stand out to me, above everything else, that i could see. I also began to notice, that the outlined edges of the bluish translucent aura field, started to enhance things, that it was in front of. I mean it would somehow, enhance the colour, and clarity of the object's, it was in front of. This is hard to explain with words, but it was like, the aura effected the clarity of the physical things, it was in front of. In the next weeks that followed, i also started to see this same bluish outline, around many different trees. I also noticed the same faded colours, further away from the trees themselves, just like i had seen on many different people, including myself. Another thing i began to notice. This mysterious energy field would be slightly different in size, and intensity, it varied from person, to person, and tree, to tree. But always the most prominent colour for me, would be the bluish, whitish one, closest to the object it was emanating from, at the time, i was viewing it. The other strange thing i began to notice was, the energy field was much harder to see, if the person, plant, or animal, was moving about at the time. I don't know, if it was harder for me to focus on, but it was definitely harder for me to see the energy field, if the viewed object was moving. Another strange fact about this phenomenon was the rain, if it was raining outside, this would greatly enhance my ability to see this energy field. It was as though, the rain would intensify it some how. I couldn't find anything about this on the internet, but the fact i could see the energy field, in much more clarity, and greater ease in the rain, meant something, i know. I'm still not sure what this means at this moment in time, but i feel, it as relevance to my life's journey. The most strangest part, started to happen about three weeks later, i started to see the same bluish whitish field, around non living things like cars, building structures, clouds, etc. This seemed to throw me quite a bit, my understanding up until this point, was that this energy field was only around living breathing things, and i was not sure at all, what all this was supposed to mean to me. I even suspected a fault with my eyes, but later discounted that theory. My eyes felt the best they had been for a long time. At this point, i had already been asking myself, lots of questions during my meditations sessions, and i knew, this was one of the questions, i really needed answering for myself. After asking only once, i received more of a inner feeling, a sense of already knowing the answer to my question. I believe we all live, in a vast invisible energy field, that surrounds everything, and also everyone. I also believe this is the field, that i have been seeing in my life for some time. I feel that this bluish, whitish field is our own body's interacting with this invisible energy field, which in turn creates this amazing visible effect of the bluish, whitish aura field, which surrounds everyone, and everything, living, and also non living. I now know, and feel inside myself, that every living, and non living thing, on and off our planet, in fact the whole universe, is a form of some kind of intelligent living energy system. This effect that i have been seeing, and maybe many others around our planet, have also been seeing for millennia, i believe holds the key to many of life's hidden, and mysterious secrets. I feel now at this point in our history, and at this exact point in time, we are at last, truly starting to understand the great importance of these many new, and strange phenomena in our lives. This bluish, whitish aura effect which i a have been seeing, or what every you want to call it, is i believe only a glimpse of this vast invisible realm, which most of us, are unable to see in our daily existence, as human beings on this planet. This is what i believe the scientist call, the hidden ninety nine percent of the universe, which they know is there, but are unable to explain its existence. This invisible field i believe is the area, from which all of creation flows, and everything we see, and understand to this day, as truly come, from this invisible energy realm. This incredible affect which the human body, and everything else we see around us, produces on this field, only proves to me, that we are all connected, and intertwined, in every way, through this invisible energy web. I believe its this web, which connects all of creation itself, this effect started to remind me in someways, to the similarities of the northern lights in our skies, when the charged particles bombard earths magnetic field, giving us a truly amazing light show. I believe the same sort of affect is happening with this invisible field, which i feel, at this point, we are all being re-awakened to on this planet. This wonderful, and mysterious energy field, fills everything we see, and also cannot see, i also feel it has a vast intelligence, guiding us all through our lives here in this vast, and amazing universe. I also believe this field, as magnetic properties of some kind. I picture it like an invisible ocean of energy, which we are all swimming around in, but are totally oblivious to this fact. I am not quite sure why, at this moment in time, i seem to have been given, this knowledge, but i know, that i am being shown this, for a greater reason, than i can understand, at this point in time. I have recently started to pick up on little clue's, in the last few days, and weeks, i have begun to notice, that when my energy levels are low, or when my body is just plain tired, i would begin to find it hard, to see the bluish, whitish aura energy field. My tiredness seem's to affect my ability to see this energy field, as though my energy levels, and also my life force, are some how directly linked, to this energy field in some way. Again i am not quite sure, what this means, but i am just trying to get everything written down into the pages of this book. I am, in no way a scientist of any kind, and i am not saying any of this as scientific fact to it, i am just trying to get these experiences down, one by one, as i am encountering them in my life's journey so far. In the last few day's, i have also started to notice, another phenomena, while meditating. I started to notice this strange affect, while i was in a state of deep meditation, and in a dark room setting. After about ten, to fifteen minutes, into my deep meditation, but not all of the time, i would start to see, with my eyes closed, flashes of brilliant light, mainly white in colour, but sometimes, blue's, and greens, even pink, and orange colours. I would also, start to get blobs of patterns, which seemed to fill my eyes, with different shapes, and flashes, the exact one's, you use to get, when you would look through a collider scope, as a child. Sometimes this would get very intense, and the only way to stop it, would be to open my eye's. On one occasion, when i opened my eyes, while still in a meditative state of mind, i seemed to notice, what looked like, beams of energy, or a faint light, which seemed to be coming from my hands. These beams seemed to be moving with my hands back and forth, up and down, in fact ever way, i would move my hands, the beams would seem to follow them. It looked like they were coming, directly from the palms of my hands, in some way. These light beams, also seemed to extend all the way across the room, it was like a science fiction movie, my hands really had some sort of energy, emanating from them. I felt like one of the x-men, it was really strange to see at first. This was the first time, i had really been in a deep meditative state of mind, with my eyes open, i would always usually keep them shut, which was the way, i had been learned through the many books, i had already read. In the days, and weeks that followed, i would start my meditating session, with my eyes closed as usual, but i would always be waiting for what i now called the signal, which was the flashing lights, followed by the collider scope blobs. I would still watch them for a while, until they began to get to intense, almost blinding me, with my eyes shut. At first though, they were actually quite nice, and had a mystifying feel to them, i began to start seeing other strange phenomena with my eyes open in the weeks, that followed. These were, what i would call, dancing clouds of whitish gas like shapes. They seemed to dance around me where i was lay. It looked, and felt like it had intelligence to it, of some kind. The first few times i had experienced this, i was quite frightened to say the least. But i knew inside me, that what ever it was, it was not here to harm me in anyway. These whitish clouds, which i was seeing, was very faint at first, but in the weeks that followed, they where more defined, and at some points, in my meditation session, they would come so close to my face, i felt sure i could feel them touching me. My body, would get goose bumps all over it, and every hair on my head, felt like it had stood on end, my whole body, felt engulfed by a unknown energy source. My body also felt as though it was being lifted in some way, it was a really strange feeling to say the least. In the weeks, and months that followed, i really started to study the mist like substance, while in a deep meditative state of mind. I noticed that it seemed to dance, and swirl, in all different patterns, and random directions. It had a definite intelligence to it, i was sure of it. I would begin to put my hands into the swirling clouds of mist, the mist would then, start to interact with my hands. It would start to swirl around my hands, and when i would move my hands, the mist would then start to disperse itself. Then i would return my hand to its original position, and the mist would start to form, and whirl, around my hand's again. There was no other explanation for this, it must of been under some sort of intelligent control, but who's i don't know. I didn't really know what to make of the these strange, and new occurrences in my life, i started to look about the internet, to see if this was a common occurrence while meditating. I did find a few instance's, of people around the internet, mentioning a very smilier phenomena in their meditations. But i can not be sure, if it was the same thing, that i was experiencing in my meditative state of mind. Most of these experience's that i was reading about, were on different forums, so i had no way to clarify, any of them, and i was unable to get into contact with the person, who had posted the original message. It seemed like i was definitely alone on this one, i felt there was no way, i could mention these new experience's, to any of my family, they would of locked me up for sure. Its quite a lonely feeling inside, to have all these new, and amazing experiences, and not be able to share many of them. I think this is one of the many reasons, i feel i need to write this book. I know there is more people, like myself, around this planet, going through exactly, or very similar experiences as i am, and also feeling quite alone. I hope that this book will help many of them, to not feel so alone, and be able to use this book as a reference, and guide, through their own life's journey. Even though many of my new experiences, at first have been quite frightening to me, and not knowing what to make of them at all. But there was always a sense on inner knowing, that everything was always part of my life's journey, and i needed many of these new experiences, to understand, who i truly was. Getting back to these new phenomena which were now becoming a part of my daily meditation sessions, and were also showing me a part of life, that i would of never imagined possible, only a few years before this point in my life. As the week's went by, i am not sure if my imagination, or maybe my human brain was starting to play tricks on me, but in my latest meditation sessions, i was starting to see in the misty shapes, and whitish clouds, what looked awfully like human faces. This was in no way frighting to me, it was quite the opposite, it was more a comforting thing. I never seen the faces every time, but every once in a while, a very well defined face, just seemed to appear from inside mist. I again do not know what to make of this, but i suspect that this is again, a part of this intelligent field, that surrounds us all, and for what ever reason, i feel it is trying to communicate to me in some way. Maybe trying to answer some of my many questions, that i have been asking myself lately. I now believe that these phenomena, are at first linked, to the deep meditative states of mind, and only become visible at a time in your life, when you are fully ready to accept these as part of your life. I continued to interact with the mist, on many more of my meditation sessions, in fact i began to look forward to my meditation sessions more than usual. It was like having a meditation partner, in the room with me, as strange as that may sound to the reader. Some weeks went by, and i began to notice, and catch glimpses of something out of the corners of my eyes, while just going about my daily life routines. What i began to discover, was the same mist, that i was seeing in the dark room, while in a meditative state of mind, i was now seeing the same mist like substance, in the day time, while in my normal waking state of mind. It looked slightly different in the light, it was almost transparent, but if i put the slightest bit of consternation into it, i could then see it as a whitish transparent mist, swirling in the same patterns, as it did, in my night time meditation sessions. The second time it happened to me, i was then one hundred percent sure, it was the same mist, but in a day light environment. I was in my back garden, relaxing on a chair, it was beautiful sunny day, and in a moment of a slight daydream, i slowly caught a glimpse of the misty substance again. It past by, both of my eyes, just like it had done, a few days before, but just like before, in the day time environment, it didn't look misty at first, but instead it looked like a transparent cloud, or it had transparent properties to it. I again found that when the mist cloud passed in front of a physical object, it seemed as though it distorted the object slightly, but it also seemed to enhance the colours of the physical object, that was in view. I mentioned this same phenomena earlier in the chapter, with the bluish whitish, aura close to our bodies, this also seemed to give the same affect. At this point i was wondering if i had some sort of problem with my eyes, i knew that my eyes had deteriorated slightly, from my younger days, but at my last eye test, i was still achieving 20/20 on the vision charts. But i still thought that my eyes maybe playing some sort of tricks on me, causing these strange new visions. I then booked an eye exam, as soon as possible at my local opticians, of course i didn't mention these strange new visions, for obvious reasons. I just explained, that i wanted to have a routine eye exam. Even though i knew deep down, my eyes were fine, i still felt, that i needed to have this eye test for myself, to put my mind at ease. There were two options, the optician gave me, a routine standard check, or i could pay extra, and have a more extensive check of my eyes. I choose the more extensive check, so i could be sure, that there was no fault with my vision. After spending nearly fourty five minutes, inside the opticians, and various test on both of my eyes, both eyes were tested ok, no problems at all, and i was just about able to achieve 20/20, on the vision charts. But i already knew this deep down, this only confirmed to me, that these many strange, and new experiences, that had been a part of my life, for the best part of three months, was one hundred percent real. This was another exciting, and new part to my life, and i was embracing it, with my arms, and mind wide open. I also feel that my mind was beginning open to many new idea's, and different possibilities about life itself. At this point, i began to look forward, to what was waiting for me in the many months to follow, in my mysterious, and magical life's journey so far.

CHAPTER 14

Life Strings

I did not know yet, but there were more strange events on the way to me, and they seemed to becoming thick and fast, at this time, in my life. It was on a regularly monday morning at work, i was standing in the large open garage door way, where we drove all of the vehicles into our workshop, for repairs. It was just like i had done, on every other morning, nothing seemed out of the ordinary at all, it was just another monday morning at work. I felt in a great mood, the sun was shinning brightly, and i could feel its warmth cover my entire face. The sun was so bright, i started to squint my eyes slightly. I could still see the gorgeous blue sky, and also the many fluffy clouds that filled it, but then another strange set of events started to occur. While i was still squinting my eye's, i started to notice in my right eye, hundreds, or maybe thousands of transparent little particles, which i can only describe as little wriggling worms, or pieces of tiny glittering threads of string, moving very fast, and in many different directions. They seemed to resemble worms, or pieces of string. At first, i thought it was a trick of the sun, so i kept on looking, and the more i concentrated, and looked for them, the more i could see them, now in both of my eyes. With my first observations, i could only seem to see them, in what i call, bright sunshine, but they were definitely there, one hundred percent. At this point, i again checked to see, if i could see them in my left, and right eye, and i could, they were visible, in both of my eye's. Wow!, they were definitely there, hundreds, or maybe thousands of them. They looked transparent, and slivery in colour, they almost seemed to glisten in some way. I rubbed my eyes again, and again at first, two or three times, just to make sure, it wasn't a trick of the bright sunshine. I even attempted to view them, on many different days, and they were always there. I found out, that all i needed, to see this amazing new phenomena in my life, was a brightish day, with whitish clouds, or a clear blue background. To see them, i would look right into the brightness of the sky, and start to squint my eyes very slightly. This would stop, any of the sun's brightness, from damaging my eyes. Eventually this new phenomena, would begin to come into view, in both of my eyes. It was another truly amazing sight for me, what were these new, and magical things, that i was now seeing. I thought to myself, why haven't i noticed them before, why can i see them now, at this point in my life. I Knew that i had squinted my eyes, thousands of times in the past, but never had i seen anything like this, when looking in to the bright sky, on a sunny day. I cannot explain what this is, but again, i feel its something, that i had to see, and also something, i needed to share with all of you, reading this book now. Please again, don't just take my word for it, you must try this for yourself, it gives you a feeling of knowing, that there is something much greater, than just our earthly lives, here on this planet. You start to get a magical new feel, and understanding about life, you also begin to develop, and unquenchable thirst for knowledge, and truth. At this point i was still total fascinated by all of these new enigmas in my life, especially these new string like worms, which i had witnessed with my very own eyes. But i was still feeling quite isolated, from the many people around me, i felt i couldn't tell anybody, about these exciting discoveries in my life. I will be honest, i am still finding it quite hard, to take in all of these amazing new discoveries in my life, i feel truly blessed, to be given access to these many new, and magical wonders about life. These new feelings, and discoveries, have begun to open my mind, to new dimensions of thought, also giving me a new, and wonderful prospective on life, as a whole, thank you. Everyone of these new areas in my life, has captivated me beyond my wildest dreams. I feel so blessed beyond words, that i am being shown these many secrets about life itself. I again needed to see, if i could find any information, regarding these new worm like strings, that i had begun to see. I needed to see if anybody else, was able to see this strange new phenomena in my life. I again began to search many of the internet sites, trying to find any information, i could, regarding these string like worms, that had entered into my life's journey, for a unknown reason, at this time. I felt i was again shown them for a reason, that i am not yet clear on. I searched for many nights on my computer, but i couldn't seem to find anything, about them at all, or anything even resembling them. I felt a bit disappointed at first, but later thought this only seemed to deepen the mystery for me, which only excited me further in the end. What were these, amazing little things, i just at to find, some sort of an answer, to my questions. I again meditated on the question, and then decided to see if the answer would come to me. At that point, i decided to give up looking for a few weeks, then a couple of weeks later, i just seemed to stumble across youtube video, while surfing the internet. I am still not sure to this day, how i arrived at the page, but the important thing is, i did. The video i came across, was about an amazing man, called Edward Leedskalnin, who built an amazing coral structure, called The Coral Castle in Florida USA. The reason i mention this here, and feel that it is relevant to my book, are as follows. Edward in a interview, or conversation with somebody over the years of is life, also mentioned these strange structures, which you can see in bright sunlight, and with a slight squinting of the eyes. He said that they were the secret to all life. I was again truly astonished, that i had been guided to this information, when i had been looking for some clarification on what i was seeing. I felt as though my question, had been answered, i also felt a sense of relief, that they had been seen before by somebody else, especially by such an intelligent human being, has Edward Leedskalnin was. Edward also talked about the fact, he knew the secrets of The Great Pyramids of Gizza. This also fascinated me, because Edward, was supposed to have built coral Castle alone, with the help of nobody else, using just a simple block and tackle device. This seemed to defy, all law's of physics, and common sense, some of the amazing structures that Edward built on his own at Coral Castle, consisted of Coral blocks weighing over thirty tones in weight, and were also gigantic in size. If these structures were built today, it would take the efforts of many men, and numerous machines to achieve this amazing feat of engineering genius. This one fact alone, proved to me that Edward Leed skalnin, was truly in the possession of an amazing secret, lost many thousands of years before, and also known, by the great builders of the pyramids of Egypt, and also the many other temple builders, from around our great planet, many thousands of years ago. Still till this very day, nobody has been able to discover how this one amazing man alone, was able to build these amazing structures. Edward also said in one of is other interviews, that the number 71296105195, was the secret to the universe. This number later turned out to be, is immigration number that he was issued on arrival to the United States of America. I believe what Edward leed skalnin was trying to tell everybody, was we ourselves, human beings are the true secret to the universe, and we are the key, to all of creation as we know it. I feel, i have a sort of connection to what he also witnessed, when he looked into the bright sunlight on a sunny day. This was just another path, that i have been guided down in this amazing life's journey, that i find my self on. I now also feel that i am being guided to life's secret's, one after another, which in turn, leads me directly to the next big discovery in my life's Journey so far. More, and more doors seemed to opening up for me, and with every one that does, i am being shown how amazing our lives can really be, if we just begin to open up our powerful minds, and look deep within our self's. Letting our hearts guide us to who we really are, guiding us to the reasons, for our being here on this planet today. I also, strongly recommend, that you take the time to read some of the amazing facts, about this truly amazing man, called Edward Leed skalnin. So you to, can discover his astonishing life achievements, so you can truly understand in your own way, how Edward Leed skalnin, seemed to know many of life's amazing secrets. I also feel, he has a lot to teach all of us, here on this planet today, thank you Edward Leed skalnin.

CHAPTER 15

Signs

O ver the next few months of my life, many other things started to appear in my life, including a set of Oracle cards, which i now use on a regular basis, for guidance when i feel, i need help with any of life situations. This simple set of cards, have become a invaluable guide in all parts of my daily life. The card set, i am using are The Power animal Cards, by Steven D. Farmer PhD. What i find amazing is, six months before this point, i would of out rightly dismissed anything like this, but here i was, using these cards, as part of my daily life routine, wow!, now thats what you call a change. After using these fantastic, and helpful cards, for two or three weeks, i began to see, some of the cards physical counterparts, the animals themselves, they started to appear in my daily life experiences. This was strange to me, because before the use of these cards, i could never remember seeing, any of these types of animals, in my daily life. I am not saying, i have never seen any of these animals, in my whole life, but there were very few times, in my thirty plus years of living, where i have seen them. I suppose many people could say, that they have always been there, and maybe i choose not to see them, ignoring that they were there all along. But i would discount that theory, because even as a young child, i have always been fascinated with animals in general, having a great love, for any sort of creature of any kind, i truly care for all animals, and i have always had a passion for all of them. So i do feel, if i ever did see, any of these animals in my daily life, i would of definitely taken notice, of them all. These new experience's, that i was now encountering in my daly life, was something totally different. It felt like, i was being guided, on a daily basis, has part of my life's journey, just like i was receiving, guidance, and answers, from my new set of oracle cards. But this time, the guidance was coming from the living animals themselves. As the weeks past, i seemed to be getting more sensitive to the message's from the many animals that surround me, in my daily life, it was as though, they were speaking to me, in some sense, as silly as that may sound. I don't mean they were speaking to me in english, i mean a sort of sensing, that they had some sort, of inner message for me. I remember arriving at work very early one morning, i had lots of paper work to do, before everybody came in for work, and also before my customers, turned up for their vehicle repairs. To my total surprise, and amazement, there right in the middle of the garage forecourt was a large Fox, the Fox was standing totally still, he or she was looking straight in to my eyes, and i was looking straight back, at his, or hers. I immediately felt a inner connection with the fox, and straight away, i instantly knew, it was another message, or guidance for me, in this part of my life's journey. We both stood there for about five minutes, but it seemed much longer than five minutes, time seemed to almost slow to a complete stop. I never uttered a word aloud, only inside my own head, saying thank you for the message, you had brought to me. Eventually the Fox turned, and casually walked away, not the slightest bit bothered about me even being there. The feelings i was getting, from the many animals that were starting to turn up, now almost on a daily basis in my life, was an overwhelming feeling of knowing, they were giving me guidance in my life's journey so far. That may sound strange, but it was almost like we were one, it didn't seem to make any difference that i was human, and they were animals or insect's, it was like, we had a universal connection, and understanding, a sort of bind if you like, to one another. That day i sat in my office, contemplating the message, the Fox had brought to me, i also thought back in my life, and as far as i could possibly remember, i had only ever seen a Fox two times, in my entire life. This was the second time, and it was very different from the first time, i could remember. After checking my new animal oracle cards for the Fox meaning, the Fox was telling me to adapt to the many changes, that was happening all around me. It was trying to tell me to be open to all possibilities, things may happen in all different ways, some i may not fully understand at this time of my life. But i must trust in all of them, and have faith, in the much bigger picture, which we sometimes cannot see. I must try not to fight the changes that are in coming in my life, and let myself be open to all possibilities. This was amazing, and matched my life perfectly at this time. I was asking myself all sorts of questions, and needing many more answer's, this information seemed to turn up, just at the right time for me. The information i received from the Fox, seemed to totally reassure me in all areas of my life, at this time. In the weeks that followed, i also started to see, many other animals, on a regular basis. The one i seemed to see the most, was a little Robin Red Breast, which always seemed to attract my attention, from what ever i was doing at the time, This little bird would always stop me, dead in my tracks, by singing a lovely peaceful song. It felt so strange, i would first here the robin at my house, when i would awake early in the morning. We have many trees around my house, and even though i could always here this amazing little bird, sometimes i could never actually see it with my eye's. I would then, on arriving at my works, later that morning, here the same peaceful song, it was truly amazing, and magical to here this same lovely peaceful song. I still don't know to this day, if this was actually the same Robin Red Breast, from my house, but i like to think that it was. I also feel, deep within myself, this was the same Robin Red Breast, in both locations. At my works there isn't many tree's, and the Robin Red Breast, would be in the same tree everyday, right outside the large garage doorway entrance. It seemed to arrive, at the same time everyday, it would arrive first thing in the morning, then again about two o'clock in the afternoon, both times singing away, for at least twenty minutes. When it did arrive, i would stop what ever i was doing, if it was possible at that time, and walk outside, and there it was, day after day, in a tree right outside the garage doorway. My family, and colleagues thought it was quite funny, that i was so fascinated by this little bird, but i knew inside me, that this little bird, had a very big meaning to me, at this part of my life's journey. On a few occasions, when i did get down, or stressed at work, i would hear its beautiful song coming from outside, and everything including the stress seemed to completely melt away from my whole body. On many other occasions, when leaving my works for home, it would also be there, on the fence singing its same happy song. The frequency of seeing this little bird, was starting to truly amaze me. These many meetings, with this truly astonishing little bird in my life, have carried on right up to my present day, which is strange in itself. I have now installed a bird feeding tray at my works premises, as a sort of thank you. Everybody at work thinks I'm mad, but thats ok, they don't understanding this little birds meaning in my life, at this point in time. Not all the animal meanings, was in my Oracle cards, so i googled most of them. The meaning of the little Robin Red Breast, seemed to be a sign of new beginnings, and Spiritual awakening, and at this time in my life, all of this made perfect sense to me. I have decided to included a small passage below, that i feel describes in my own words the message, that i feel this little bird was giving to me at this moment in my life's journey. There are also many other meanings that are readily, and also freely available to anyone searching for the spiritual meaning, of this amazing little bird, i hope you like mine.

The Robin Red Breast, my be small in size, but when it arrives in our lives, it brings with it, a very powerful, and also important message for the direction of our lives. It also brings a message of new growth, and new beginnings. It's letting us know, that there will soon be big changes taking place within our life, its asking us to have faith, and let go of old outdated belief's, letting in new feelings of joy, happiness, and love. It also brings with it a message of new spiritual growth, and rebirth, letting us know that we must trust in god on our new path of winding discoveries, that lie's ahead of us. It also reminds us that we must control our new feelings, and emotions, giving them a chance to show their true meanings towards our new path in life.

The next most amazing message, i got on my life's journey, which i feel, i must also share with you, was not from the animal kingdom, but from a tiny little insect. This message turned out to be more astounding, than i could of ever imagined, in my wildest dreams. Even though this message came to me, from one of the smallest little insect's i know on our planet today, the message it had for me, packed by far the most power-fullest punch. Over the many years of my life, i have come across many of these colourful, and truly beautiful little insect's, but this particular incident, turned out to be, a real turning point for me on my life's journey so far. What really surprised me again with these many new events in my life, was their truly mystical nature, again giving me a sense of how truly magically our lives really are, here on this planet today. This latest incident happened to me, when i was fitting a new outside light, to the door way of my house. Wendy, my wife was helping me at the time to put it up. It was such a beautiful day, the sun was shinning really brightly, i had a wonderful feeling inside of myself, it turned out to be a very hot day, even though, it was still early on in the morning. I was about half way through putting up the light, when Wendy came out of the house, with a cool drink for me, she said to me in a startled voice, your covered in lady birds. Because i had been so tied up, with fitting the new outside light, i never even noticed the Lady Birds on me, i looked down, and i actually was covered all over my body, with at least seventy red little Lady Birds, she wasn't exaggerating at all. They were all over my pants, and the top part of my body. This was the first time, i had ever seen, so many Lady Birds together in one place. Before today, i had only ever seen them in one's, and two's. The other strange fact was, a few months before this strange incident, i would of just panicked, and probably knocked them all of me, but again, my inner reaction to this incident, was one of calmness, and knowing, that this was another important sign for me, on my life's journey so far. I was completely astonished with myself, about the calmness, i was showing with this strange event. For quite a while, i just stared in amazement at all them covering my body, and again just like the Fox, i knew this was a another sign for me. At this point, i again seemed to get the strange sensation, of time slowing down, just like it had done with the fox, that morning, at my works. Time just seem to stop, what seemed like ten minutes to me, was really only a minute or two, then the Lady Birds just seemed to disappear from me, just like they seemed to appear from nowhere. I have got to be honest, at this point i was quite taken back by the whole incident, even my wife Wendy, was quite shocked in a nice way, from what had just taken place, before both of our eyes. They all just seemed to vanish into thin air, as quickly as they had appeared. Even though Wendy didn't know, that it was a message, or a sign which i immediately picked up on, she still knew this was quite out of the ordinary. She didn't say much after the event, but it definitely left her thinking, and she was quite, for some time after the event. This give me a happy feeling inside myself, because it had been very hard for me, for sometime, trying to find a way of sharing these many new things in my life, with the people who were so special to me. I truly hoped, and also felt that this was a little sign for Wendy has well, and not just for me, just maybe it would open Wendy's mind a little, giving me more of a chance, to share this amazing knowledge with her, and the rest of my family. I have included my own explanation, below that i felt described the real meaning that the Lady Birds, was trying to give me at that exact moment in my life's journey. I feel these few words below, describe exactly what was happening in my life, at that very moment in time. I truly hope that these incidents will give you the inspiration in your own life's journey, and maybe you will start to see the many message's, from nature which you may have been missing in your own life. I believe that when you truly start to open up yourself, to these many pointers, and message's that life is giving you on a daily basis, through the many animals, insects, and also the many other livings things on our planet. You yourself will come to understand that we are truly not alone, and that our lives here on earth, are part of a much, much bigger picture.

The Lady Bird seems to appear in our lives, to bring us a message of rebirth, renewal, and also regeneration, a renewal of the spirit within us all. It also brings us hope, on our new path of discovery, giving us the faith to embark on the new challenges that we may face in our journey of life. It reminds us to be fearless in these challenges, that may lie ahead on our life's path. It also reminds us to let go, and let life happen, try not to worry to much, let the divine will guide us on our path in life. It reminds us to be joyful in life, be grateful for what we already have in our lives. It also brings us a message of new abundance arriving in all area's of our life, filling our hearts with a feeling of love, and happiness. It reminds us of our commitments to family life, the love, and bond between family members. I truly feel that this little tiny insect, has a very powerful message for us all.

Before i close this chapter, i feel that i must mention this one more incident, i feel that i would like to mention them all to you, but i feel that this would fill a book in its own right, and this being my first book, i am not really sure how long it should be. That aside, i feel this to important to leave out, so here goes. It wasn't long after the Ladybird incident, that i started to notice Spiders everywhere, and also their webs everywhere i looked. This didn't seem, to unusual at first, but after a few weeks of this, i couldn't ignore it anymore. I will be honest with you, i have never been a lover of Spiders, so this was quite unsettling at first, they seemed to be everywhere i was. I would pick something up, and there one would be, sitting there under the object i had just lifted, i would get into my van or car, there one would be, sometimes sitting in a web. If this wasn't strange enough, days later, i was painting my children's outside play area. As i sat there painting away, high up on the roof frame, a quite large Spider came very close to me. It seemed to crawl right to my hand, i never panicked, and just left my hand there. It then moved near the wet painted area, i thought it would get stuck in the wet paint, and possibly die, so i tried to divert it from harm. It then made its way to a side structure of the frame, and to my complete astonishment, the Spider started to spin a web, right in front of my very eye's. I mean i could see the actual web be spun from its abdomen area, what i was seeing was truly amazing, it was in crystal clear detail, the sun was shinning bright, i felt completely mesmerized by what was happening, right in front of my eyes. I sat there for some thirty minutes, i think i never really kept track of the time, it felt just like the times before, when time seemed to stand still. This truly astonished me to watch how this little creature, spun this vast complex web, right in front of me. When the Spider finished, it seemed to position itself right in the middle of the web, and lay there motionless, probably exhausted from its vast achievement. I wasn't sure what the message was for me at this time, but days later in my mothers garden, the same thing happened, another Spider spun a even larger web in front of me, and did the exact same thing, stayed motionless in the middle of the web at the end of it. Something inside me, told me that the message, was one of hard working, and eventually reaping the rewards from my tireless efforts. Again this seemed to ring true to me, i was definitely working hard at trying to adapt to the many changes, and different direction's so far on my life's journey.

CHAPTER 16

Looking Inward And Healing Myself

As the months progressed, i started turning my attention more, and more inward, by this i mean, i started to focus much more of my attention on my inner being, some people call this the human soul, or spirit. All i know its, the part of yourself, that does all of the work, behind the scenes, staying in the shadows of our human existence. I was starting to realize, that i could really use this new found knowledge, and power in so many ways, and areas of my life, the list was truly endless. I just needed to use my imagination, a little bit more. The first thing i wanted to do, was apply this knowledge, to any outstanding health issues, that were affecting the quality of my life, at this time. I think everybody at sometime in their lives, as needed to deal with some sort of health issues, from minor ones, to the more serious life threatening ones. I feel that i have been very fortunate in my life, leading a very healthy life. But i was not totally free, from the many things that can affect, the human body, and also the human mind. By far the most problematic of these for me, had been my back, it had been the biggest problem in my life, and also the longest standing health issue, that i have needed to deal with in my life time, so far. I think a lot of my back problems, have been caused in part, by the many years of weight lifting that i had done, from a very early age. I was introduced to weight training, from the early age of twelve, by my uncle, and i immediately fell in love with it. I still practice weight training now and then, but it is not part of my daily fitness routine, and at this point, i only use small weights for lifting, and training with. I first started to feel pain in my back, around ten years earlier, it eventually, and gradually built up into a constant problem for me in my life. The research i had done, on my back problem over the years, seemed to point to back injuries, being one of the most common problems, across the human race as a whole. I knew that i wasn't the only one, and there were also millions of other people all over the planet, dealing with the same problems as me, day, after day. To date, i had already tried a lot of different avenues, including chiropractors, physio therapy, exercise, and many other different exercise devices. I also looked to a more desperate measure, looking into the drastic avenue of surgery, to fix this problem once and for all, but none of the above, ever seemed to be the right option for me. I did get some temporary relief over the years, from the many different chiropractors, that i visited over the many years of my life, but this relief from the pain, would only last for a few days, or sometimes only hours. I have already mentioned in the previous chapters, what a life changing experience, it had already been to find out, and already use some of these very powerful secrets, that life as already given to me, including the very special, and ancient art of yoga. I cannot tell you, the difference this has already made to my bodies health, as a whole, including the health of my back. It as cut down the aching, and the constant pain, that i have been suffering with for so long. This is a true miracle in its self, and i am truly grateful for everything yoga as given back to me, in my life. But i also, wanted to build on that success, and the gift that yoga had already given back to me, my health. So again, i started to apply all the new things, that i had already discovered, and learned about how life really works, seeing if i could end my back problems for good. What i had learned, over the last year or so, had really turned my understanding of this world, completely upside down. Everything, i had ever been told through my life, from the very beginning to nearly the present day, was all being totally re-written again for me. I didn't accept, most of this new information as fact over night, some of the new information, i was learning about, seemed to far fetched to be true, was all this really possible. I really needed to look deep within my inner self, turning the impossible, into the possible. It just seemed so far off, what i had thought life to truly be, and believe me, this took a great leap of faith, and courage on my part, to even consider, most of these new ways of thinking, and understandings about life. But once, i really looked deeper into these new understandings about life, that had began to take over me, i knew with all my heart, they were the truth, and i have never needed to question them since, neither have i ever wanted to. I now have total faith, in these many new understandings about our humans lives. Even Science, was now beginning to confirm, many of these new findings to be true. What we think of as solid objects in our physical world, the many different things, that fill our daily lives, the chair we sit on, the house you live in, the car you drive, even down to our own physical human bodies, is not solid at all. Everything we see, is made up from pure vibrational energy waves. I know at first this may sound really strange, and crazy, even hard to believe at first. This understanding also took me with great surprise, and shock at the beginning. I don't think, that any of these new understandings about life come easy, and they also take along time to deal with, on a mental, and emotional level to. At first its like a roller coaster ride of emotions, and feeling's, you try to fight them, and ignore them, fearing your sanity. But eventually, in the end, the truth shines through all of these different feeling's, and emotions, ending with a inner understanding, of certainty, and fact, that these new feelings, are a total truth. The more i studied this, and researched the available data, which is out there, for everybody else to see for themselves. It began to leave me in no doubt, of the many implications, that these amazing, and great new understandings of our world, would eventually have, on every human being, on our planet today. Some of the greatest minds of our time, are now beginning to prove, that many of these new understandings of our world, are one hundred percent scientific fact, at this very moment now. The world we see, taste, smell, and touch, is really just an illusion of our powerful human mind, or human consciousness. This maybe quite a frightening thought, to many people at first, but this should not be the case. What as truly amazed me, with all of these new discoveries in human existence, was the amazing discovery, that our ancient ancestor, form all over the ancient world, thousands, up on thousands of years ago, knew about all of these amazing truths, and secrets about the human consciousness, even before we did. Even more spectacular, was the fact they also implemented, many of them into their daily lives. I now feel, this is how many of the ancient world's greatest, and also unexplainable structures were built. They used this powerful knowledge, to build some of the worlds greatest civilizations, that has ever lived on this planet. I now truly believe this, with all my heart, what man can conceive in his great mind, he can in turn transform his visions, into the physical plane we call our world. This great understanding means the life your living right now, is only a mirror reflection of what your are thinking, in your powerful mind, and consciousness. Meaning any circumstances in your life, from health, to wealth, love, happiness, joy, can all be changed, just with your minds thoughts, coupled with a truly burning heart desire to do so. These two powerful, and magical facts, if used correctly, will change your life, to a life of your wildest dreams. I discovered that illness, is nothing more than a disturbance, in our human energy fields, caused primarily by our thoughts, feelings, and emotions, coupled together with our past beliefs regarding our lives. I feel a lot of our health problems, start from the many emotional upsets, we begin to encounter through our lives here on this planet. I feel that we begin to store these negative emotions, in our human energy fields, and with no way to release them, they eventually lead into what we call physical illness, in our human bodies. At this point of my life's journey, i was guided to a website, on the internet, called the healing codes by Alex Lloyd PHD, which i immediately knew, was the next path in my life's journey. I jumped head first into the healing codes, because my back at the time, was still giving me a few problems, and was leaving me in some discomfort, and pain. I immediately downloaded the audio book, because at the time, that was the only option, i could get my hands on. I again, listened with great interest, with what he had to say, i also, at the same time, seemed to have stumbled across another amazing book, called Cosmic energy by Anne Jirsch, i feel i must mention this boot here, so you can discover it for yourself. Basically, the healing codes was a way of releasing stored up negative emotions from many years before. Possibly child hood memories, or traumatic events in your life, that you thought you may had forgotten all about. Only to find, that they had been there all along, hiding, and lying dormant somewhere, deep within the subconscious mind. At first i couldn't seem to relate to this at all, i knew i had a very happy, and amazing child hood, and i definitely didn't remember, any bad memories from it. Then i was thinking thoughts of, how was it possible, that my bad back, could be caused by negative memories, as old as twenty five years or more. But i was determined to listen till the end of the book, and give it a chance to explain everything to me, and i am so glad, i stuck with it. By the end of this amazing book, i had been given a new way, to release, and also remember my stored up negative emotions, and memories, by using a simple series of hand movements, and controlled thoughts. The problem was, i didn't even think, i had any negative memories stored up in my subconscious mind, but as the weeks went by, i started to unearth some very deep negative memories, which i believed, i had forgotten all about, many years before.

CHAPTER 17

Hidden memories revealed

The first hidden memory i came across, which i thought i was well and truly over, and had completely forgotten about, turned out to be exactly the opposite. I had not forgotten about this bad memory at all, i had just hidden it away, deep within my subconscious mind, where it had lay dormant for sometime, escaping my conscious mind. This memory, was from my early childhood. The incident in question, happened in the start of my early teenage years. When the healing codes, started to bring out these early traumatic memories again, from the deepest areas of my subconscious mind, i then started to realize, just how much these memories did still affect me, on a emotional level. When i started to think, and replay these event's, in my mind's eye again, even though, they were now over thirty years ago, they still affected me, as though it was happening, in the present moment now. The event in question, happened one night, when i was just thirteen years of age. I was making my way home alone, from a night out with my friends, just like i had done many times before. I had only just said goodbye to my friends, and was thinking, and having a little laugh to myself, about the good night, i had just been having with my best friends. When i eventually approached my house that evening, i seemed to get a very uneasy feeling, in the pit of my stomach, i am still not sure to this day, if this was some sort of warning for me, like a sort of sick sense, but unfortunately if it was a warning, i completely ignored it, at my own peril. What i did not realize at the time, i was being followed by a very dangerous man, who only days before, had been arrested by the police, for harassing young boys, in the local area, where i lived. At that time, being a local boy myself, i had heard about this man, he had made a name for himself, around all of the surrounding towns, and cities. On arriving at my house, i went straight around the back of the house, through the garden, and shed area, like i had done hundreds of time's before. This was where my mum, always kept the back door key, for me and my brother Steven. We had already lost so many house keys, she felt this was the only way, that she could stop us loosing the house key's. She would leave it under the same plant pot every time. As i opened the back gate, and headed into the darkness of the back garden, i made my way straight to the plant pot, to retrieve the hidden door key. I searched around in darkness, for the backdoor key, i suddenly heard a sound from behind me, a sort of scuffling of feet, as i turned around to look, to my complete and utter horror, there was a man standing there, staring straight at me. Unfortunately this particular night, with my house being in complete darkness, i knew straight away, i was in big trouble, the house being in complete darkness, was a sign to me, that none of my family members were in the house to help me. This man, was standing at least six feet tall, or maybe even taller, or at least, it seemed that way at the time. I was stood there in complete darkness, and the most frightening thing of all was, he just stood there, not saying a word, looking straight at me, and not even seeming to blink. I stood there for what seemed like an eternity to me, thinking about what this man was going to do to me. He seemed to stand there looking straight at me, with no emotions on his face what so ever. I felt completely frozen in the spot, where my feet were stood, not knowing what to do for the best. This stand off with him, seemed to last forever. By this time, all sorts of things was going through my mind, was he going to kill me, or try to molest me, was i going to survive this. At first i tried to shout, but nothing seemed to come out of my mouth, it felt so dry. I then knew that i needed to do something fast, he sort of shuffled a few steps towards me, immediately i stumbled backwards. Somehow i plucked up the courage, to try and get past him, i seen a gap to the left of him, and went for it, unfortunately he grabbed me, as i tried to get past him. This coming together with him, then resulted in a fierce, and violent struggle. I found myself battling for my survival, fortunately for me, by this time, as i mentioned in previous chapters, i had already been weight training for sometime, and i was already showing big gains in strength, and size for my early age. Luckily for me at this time, i think this new strength, that i had gained from weight training, definitely took him somewhat by surprise. I was putting up quite a fight, like anybody else would, who felt that their life, was in grave danger. I then felt my body tiring, from the constant struggle with this stranger. At that moment, i could hear a passing crowd of people, making their way past my house. I immediately let out, large screams, and cry's for help, it was that loud, i thought the whole street would here me. It seemed my voice had finally returned, just when i needed it the most. My screams for help seemed to panic the man, he tried to grab my mouth to keep me quite, but as he did, he lost his tight grip on me, i immediately escaped, and made my way to, and through the garden gate, where a crowd of people had now gathered, hearing my loud screams for help. As i reached the crowd, i explained what had just happened, the police were immediately contacted, and i felt a sense of relief come over my entire body. Even though i was still shaking, and bleeding from the thirty minute, or so struggle with this stranger. I knew at that very moment, that i had been very fortunate, to escape this man, with myself completely intact in every way, only suffering a few cuts, and minor bruises. After a later discussion with the police about this man, i then knew things could have turned out a lot worse for me. Just after the attack, i didn't really feel as though, i had been attacked, i tried to put a bit of a brave face on it, telling my family, and friends it wasn't such a big deal. But weeks after the attack, i started to feel very affrayed, and i didn't want to be alone, or by myself anymore. I even stopped going out for sometime with my friends, fearing it may happen to me again. It took me quite sometime, to get back to a normal thirteen year old boy routine again. My family were very supportive at the time, and i thought i was well over the incident, but the healing codes, started to unearth some very deep emotional memories regarding this attack, from many years earlier in my life. I now know for certain that these traumatic memories were still there all along, but buried deep within my subconscious mind, for all that time. I truly thought within myself, that this incident from so many years before, was completely forgotten. But the healing code's, brought it all to the forefront of my mind's thoughts again, and when it did, with the help of the healing codes, i began to confront it head on, not letting it disappear again, in to the deep depth's of my subconscious mind. With the help of The Healing Codes, i began to completely let go of this negative, and traumatic memory completely. The total acceptance of this dark memory felt amazing to me, it was like, i had been carrying a fifty kilogram ruck sack on my back for all these years, with out even realizing it. I felt that when this memory was finally released, and confronted, and brought back from the depth's of my subconscious mind. The feeling of weight, on my back that accompanied this dark memory, seemed to leave my entire body. The other amazing effect of this memory release, was a instant relief in my back pain, which i had endured over the years of my life. I am not trying to say, it was cured in a instant, but from that day on, and every day since, i seem to be on a road, to a complete, and amazing recovery of my back, and also many other little health issues, that i have seemed to put up with, over the many years of my life so far. This amazing, and simple method, seemed to be healing me, when all of the other options i had tried, over the many years of my life, had seemed to completely fail me. I also went on to release many other memories from my sub conscious mind, i also thought many of these memories were long forgotten to, but they were just hidden away, lurking within the deep depths of my subconscious mind. But i feel this is beyond the scope of this book, maybe in the future, i will write another book, just on the healing techniques, i have encountered, and also learned on this amazing life's journey so far. I now know, and feel, with all my heart that anything is truly possible in this life, including the healing of our earthly bodies. We just need the knowledge, and faith to do this, and i hope this book, i am writing now, will give you the tools, and encouragement to do so. Embarking you on your own life's journey of discovery, giving you the tools to heal your own life, if needed. At this point i would just like to touch on a book, i have just read over, and over again, the book is by Anne Jirsch, called Cosmic Energy. I found some truly inspirational reading, and also great healing techniques, within the pages of this valuable book, please take the time to read, and enjoy this amazing book yourself.

CHAPTER 18

Discovering TFT

Looking further into what i now call the healing part of my life's journey, i started to come across many different approaches to healing the human body, and mind. As i continued to research the fascinating subject of healing, i came across another fairly new technique, which again seemed to stand out to me, more than any of the others i was reading about at this time, just like the healing codes had done, only a few months before. This revolutionary healing technique, which is now quite widely spread, and seems to be sweeping over, every part of our planet, is an amazing but again simple technique to use on yourself. The Healing technique which i refer to, is called TFT, Short for Thought Field Therapy. This was founded by Dr Robert J Callahan PhD, and was again, another healing technique, that had a instant, and profound effect on me. I found it very similar to The Healing Codes, that i used only a few months before, to help rid myself, of some very dark, and hidden memories from depth's of my subconscious mind. But this new technique turned out to be a lot more powerful for me, and the dramatic results were also instantaneous, in their affect on my body. I mean the healing affect happened, at the exact time, i used the technique for what ever problem i felt i needed it for, wow!, it really did feel like a miracle cure. Again this technique was so easy to use on yourself, i also thought it was quite fun to, well it felt like fun for me, you will have to judge that for yourself, if you do decide, to look into using this for yourself, which i sincerely hope you do. I hope that it brings you, the same miraculous results, that it has done for me, in my life, so far. This method of healing works by tapping different energy points on your body in a patterned sequence, designated by the type of problem, that you are using it for. This revolutionary treatment can be used, to release so many things from simple phobias, pain, stress, and anxiety, and also many other human health conditions. The most amazing part of this powerful technique for me, was the short time it took, to do the tapping treatments on yourself, or others. It was no more than five, or six minutes to do each of the tapping sessions. This resembled the healing codes in so many ways, but for me TFT, turned out to have a very powerful effect on my body, and also my mind, it was also fun and very exciting to use. But that in no way, takes any of the shine of the Healing codes for me, i am still truly grateful with all my heart, for what the healing codes, had already done for me in my life, and they would always, from this point on, be a part of my life forever, staying in my healing tool kit. That is the true beauty of this amazing life we live, we have our free will, we can explore all different avenues, choose our own unique experiences, play out our own destinies, choose what is right for us, not for anybody else. You may find in your own life's journey, that you come across some other totally different healing technique, which may turn out to be, the one to heal your life. That's why life is so fantastic, we all get to choose our own path in this life, i can not stress enough, the amazing effects that TFT has had on my day to day life, nothing short of miracle. Even with my new found knowledge about every area of human life, i was still like everybody else in the world, just living a normal day to day life, this routine eventually, no matter how hard we try, leads us to get a little stressed, or sometimes very stressed. I am afraid to say, modern life at some stage, will lead us all into a state of being over worked, eventually heightening our stress levels, and in some cases, leading to complete exhaustion of our human bodies. Our bodies eventually just start to lock up, and become unresponsive, in many way's, leaving most of us, feeling not so great at all. What i found though, completely amazed me, i found out just by doing a five minute TFT tapping sequence a day, on various energy points around my body, would instantly pick me up, and also re-energize my whole body, and mind. This was instantly life changing for me, i started to use this magical technique every single day of my life, i began to find out, through my research on the internet, that TFT, was going through what i call, an evolutionary expansion in the ways, that it could be used on the human body, and also the human mind. Many different People from all over the planet were evolving TFT, to be used on just about anything. Again the great human imagination, was taking this magical gift given to us from the genius, Dr Robert J Callahan PhD, and taking it to new evolutionary heights. New adaptions, and editions to TFT, were going to make TFT, a new global tool for the fight against human illness, both physical, and mentally. I hope that Dr Robert J Callahan PhD, is really proud to have started a new revolution, in the healing of the human being, has a species, thank you, with all my heart. I started to show my friends, and family this powerful tool for them to use in their life. It was to simple, and powerful not to. That was the beauty of this tool, it was so easy to learn, and you could use it just about anywhere, you had a spare few minute's. I started to use it half way through the day, while sitting at my desk at work, i would give myself a TFT Tapping session, and this would boost my energy levels immediately. Believe me, thats a powerful feeling, being able to tap into a reserve hidden energy bank within myself wow!!!, but like everything else on this life's journey, it all seemed to be leading me somewhere, and in a definite direction towards healing. I felt this was only the beginning for me, and i had already found out from two other sources along my life's journey, that one of my possible life purposes, here on planet, this time around, could be a career in healing, of some kind. Then the bells started to ring in my head again, this path, i was on, seemed to match exactly, what the medium had already said to me, when i visited her, only a six months before this point in my life's journey. She said to me on that day, and the words still ring loud in my ears, that she felt that i had the energy of healer of some kind. Even though at the time, i didn't seemed to fully understand the importance, or the direction that this statement may send my life on, i still seemed to take note of what she had said to me. But i just put it to the back of my mind at that time. Its only now again, at this point in my life's journey, have i fully come to understand, and feel that healing, may have always been, the missing part of life. But it was still only early days for me, in this new avenue of thinking, and i feel that i was only just starting to heal my own body, and mind. I instantly knew this to be just another pointer for me to follow, and investigate in my life's journey so far. I also continued my research, completely fascinated, by how these simple techniques could change peoples lives almost instantly. I started to watch many more internet videos, and found out, that you could use TFT Therapy, with word affirmations to bring more wealth, happiness, love, joy, and peace into your life. In fact you could use this technique to change all areas of your life, and make every dream, you have ever wanted come true, including the return of your healthy body, and mind. The only limitation, is your own imagination. A few months went by with great improvements in all areas of my life, including my general well being, even my general happiness with life greatly improved. I also continued with my love of meditation, incorporating a bit of TFT mixed in with it, if your don't try, you'll never know ha ha!!!.

Chapter 19

Discovering Mystical Egypt

In the weeks that followed, out of the blue, i seemed to fall into a new passion, these new feelings seemed to appear from no where. This new passion in my life, was for the ancient land of Egypt. It all started with a set of very vivd, and strange dreams, regarding this mysterious, and ancient place. The dreams seemed to keep repeating them selfs, not every night, sometimes there would be a gap of days's, but the same dreams, would eventually return to my sleeping hours. The details were never exactly the same, but the many scenes in the dreams would always look, and feel the same to me. When i say feel, i really mean it, the dreams really did feel real to me. The dreams would be so detailed, and sometimes so intense, they would awake me from my deep sleep. At this point in my life, i had never visited ancient Egypt, and i had only ever seen pictures of the Great Pyramids of Gizza, on the many television programs, and sky documentary channels, that fill our tv screens these days. But this new, and sudden fascination seemed to completely take over me, and engulf my entire being. I would awake thinking about Egypt, and also fall asleep thinking about Egypt. As the weeks progressed, the dreams started to get more elaborate, and on awakening from my sleep, i would remember my dreams in exceptional detail. This was something new for me, before these dreams, i had never really remembered my dreams in very much detail, but now, i could recall all my dreams, with unusual detail. With this new fascination, i started to research all the information i could find out, regarding this ancient, and amazing civilization. One of the first things i came across, in my studies, about ancient Egypt, was their fascination in astrology. I have always felt a connection, with the night sky, it has always filled me, with a sense of excitement, and true mystery. I think the night sky, has a sense of intrigue, and mystery for everyone, when you look up on a clear night, it fills your entire being with a sense awe, and wonder, at its beauty. I was also amazed by the many pharaoh's, that had ruled this vast, and great land. These great men, and women, along with the masses, turned Egypt, into one of the wonders, of the ancient world. Some of the amazing structure's built by the Egyptian people, many thousands of years ago, still stand to this present day. Millions of people, from around the globe, flock to Egypt every year, to see its wonders for themselves. The further facts, that i began to uncover about this truly astonishing civilization, truly amazed me. They were so advanced for there time in history, their many building achievements, still baffle, many of the worlds scientist's, and engineers till this present day. I was finding myself, in the grip of Egypt fever. The one dream that i remember so vividly, and it was the one, that seemed to repeat itself for sometime, in the coming months of my life, began to give me the inspiration, to try and find a reason, for these strange, and mysterious dreams, that i was now having on a regular basis. I was looking for a reason, to why at this point, in my life's journey, was i having these strange dreams about this magical, and ancient place. The dream i refer to, always started with myself stood on, a large stone complex, i seemed to be standing at the top of a steep set of steps, in the middle of a complex. The complex was vast in its size, there was high walls to my left, and right. There were what i can only explain as coloured drawings, on each side of the structured walls. As the dreams repeated themselves i picked up more, and more details from them. I eventually worked out, that i was standing on some sort of temple platform. As i looked out from the platform, in front of me, there was a vast open area, where a large crowd of people were gathering. It seemed like thousands of people, were just standing there, looking straight at me. In my later dreams, the crowd seemed to be listening to me speaking. I remember shouting so loudly to the waiting crowd, that i woke myself from the dream that i was having. It seemed like i was giving some sort of speech, to the waiting crowd of people, i also seemed to be holding something in my right hand. I could never make it out, in very much detail, but it was gold in colour, and it looked like a sort of weapon, or staff. It always seemed to be in my right hand, the object i was holding was longer than my body, and at one point, i seemed to raise this staff, or weapon, into the air, almost punching the air, with a thrusting like action, while at the same time, addressing the vast awaiting crowd. At various points in the dream, the crowd would seem to burst into chants of cheering, and shouting, in a language, that i was unfamiliar with. The noise from the crowd, was truly defining to my ears, and again, this would sometimes awaken me, from my dream state. I know all this, may sound very strange to the reader of this book, but i feel deep inside myself, that there is a hidden message, or meaning to my life's journey, held somewhere within these strange, and mysterious dreams. Even though, at this point in my life's journey, i do not fully understand the significance of these dreams. I feel that they play a part in my life's Journey, and i am hoping that their reasons, will soon become clear to me, so that i may use their guidance to help me, on this life's journey, of ever expanding mystery, and discovery. With another strange set of coincidences, two years before my life's journey even started. Out of no where, i planned to have two tattoos done, with my daughter, and sons name on each of my forearms. This fact alone, is not, at all uncommon, lots of parents tattoo their children's names on their bodies, we are all so proud, to show them of to the world at large. But for some reason, which i still cannot remember, till this very day, the two tattoos, that i had done, on that day, on each of my forearms, were both done, in what i have now found out to be, ancient Egyptian hieroglyphic text. I still remember the tattoos artist comments, at the time of the tattoo, asking me where, i had located this strange art work, for the design of my tattoos. All i knew at the time was, it had come from one of the many internet site's, where you could translate all different types of languages, like english to hieroglyphic text. He said to me, in his many years of doing tattoos, this was the first one, he had ever seen like this one. At the time of my tattoos, i never even give this a second thought, i just thought they looked really cool, and both of my children would love them. I am not saying, that these two strange events are definitely related, but something inside me, is saying that they may just be. The mystery seemed to deepen further at this point, the strange dreams that i was having, seem to be happening much less frequent, but now i seemed to start seeing pyramid shapes everywhere i looked. I would also start to see programs all the time about Egypt, holiday brochures would come through the door for Egypt, i was seeing poster's about Egypt, while driving my car. It felt like, i was being bombarded by all things Egypt. In the end the pointers were again, just to strong for me, to ignore them. Even as i switched on the television at night, the very channel i selected, was a program about ancient Egypt. I just knew that, Egypt somehow, was a part of my life's journey, and i needed to start listening to the many messages, i was now receiving, on a daily basis. Until this point in my life, i had never been really interested in human history, on our wonderful planet. In fact at school, i never really paid attention to any of my history lessons. But now, i couldn't seem to get enough, of the history of ancient Egypt. It was like being back at school, doing all the research work again, but this time, i was actually interested in what i was learning, and doing, and believe me, that makes a vast difference. In the past few years of my life, it seems i have become, a great listener, and also a eager student in many new, and different subjects, that have now change my life in new, and fascinating ways. I just couldn't seem to get Egypt out of my head, at this point in my life's journey. I started reading more, and more, i also watched many more videos on the internet, about this amazingly advanced civilization. I really needed to find out, why i had been drawn to this mysterious, and magical culture. I later found out, through my many studies into this magical civilization, that they were a truly advanced civilization for their time in history, some may say, they were to advanced for their time in history. By this i mean they must have been helped in some way, or by some one, meaning off world help. Many scientist, and ordinary people from around the world, found it a complete mystery to explain, how such and ancient civilization, was able to build such elaborate, and vast structure's, with only a limited set of primitive tools, compared to today standards. But there is no need for me to cover that here, there have been many great books written regarding this subject, and i feel it would be pointless for me to fill the pages of this book with them also. But at this point, i would urge you to read some of these fascinating books, which are out there, some are truly enlightening, and have been written by some extremely cleaver people, who truly know their chosen subject's. I have now come to believe, that my connection, and also my fascination with this inspirational culture, was with their strong spiritual beliefs. Everywhere i read about this culture, every source confirmed, that they were a great spiritual people. Their civilization was built, around their spiritual beliefs, i also feel that my life's journey, has now in part, turned into a spiritual one, at this point in time. Maybe we all need aspects of spirituality in our life's journeys. What i have come to understand, with the reading, and the study of much material, from all different sources, is that we all come to a point in our lives, whether its early on in our existence, or later on towards the end of our physical lives, when we all embark on a spiritual quest, whether we are aware of it, or not. It now seems, and feels to me, that i am now at that major changing point, or cross roads in my life's journey, i now truly believe with all my heart, that i must go through these stages of spiritual evolution, to get where i want to go. Leading me down my true life's path, or life's purpose here on planet earth today. This journey, or life quest, has been called many name's, by many different cultures, all over the planet. I Feel it does not matter what we call it, but i feel that we must step into these special opportunities with open minds, embracing them into our entire being. I feel if we continue to resist, and fight the purpose we are hear for on this planet, it will in turn cause nothing but destruction, within ourselves, and make our life here on this planet, a never ending struggle, the choice is completely ours alone, our own free will, remember!!. I now believe that my health problems, relating to my physical body, over the many years of my life, were caused partially, by my constant fighting with life. I also feel that the majority of my health issues, were signs for me, letting me know, i was so far away, from my true life's path, or purpose this time around on planet earth. I feel now at this point in time, my eyes are completely wide open, to the real, and true possibilities of life, and i am finally embracing my life with open arms, and also a very open mind. Finally my body ailments are miraculously healing themselves, one after another, which i now feel is due to me letting go, of all my resistance to my life's path, here on planet earth, this time around. In the last few days i been brought back to the blue, white halo, which i have continued to see in greater abundance. Within days, i came across new information regarding this phenomena, which seemed to finally address these issue's, and started to answer the questions, that i had been asking, over the last few months of my life's journey so far.

CHAPTER 20

Orgone Energy

T he answer i received, was from the ground breaking work, of a truly brilliant scientist called Wilhelm Reich, and the subject of orgone energy. This new, and exciting information seemed to validate, what i had been seeing, over last weeks, and months of my life's journey. The research Wilhelm Reich did in his life time, was truly ground breaking in every way, he seemed so far ahead of his time. He concluded with his many years of tireless studies, including many experiments, that a blue energy field surrounded all living, and non living Matter on this planet, in fact it surrounded planet earth itself, and also filled the vast universe, and many galaxies at large. He also confirmed that the orgone energy field is everywhere, it fills every empty space we can see, and also cannot see, in fact empty space is not empty at all, it is filled with this magical blue orgone energy field. The most exciting part of his studies, showed that we as human beings, can use this energy field. It is the life force of everything, and we can use it for many different purposes, including the healing of our human bodies, which we already know, is made of pure vibrational energy. I seemed again, to be on the subject of healing. After reading more on what i believe to be, one of the most amazing, and important discoveries of the twentieth century. I now feel, and believe that Wilhelm Reich, has given us, a very big clue, and also answered one of life's greatest secrets, to who we truly are. His ground breaking discoveries were made in the 1950's, and unfortunately, at that time in history, his ideas were so far ahead of there time. This led most of the scientific community, to disregard his ground breaking work, and scientific findings. For this reason he was ridiculed, and belittled for his beliefs, and his scientific findings. This poor treatment, of such a brilliant man, eventually turned into what many called, a witch hunt, leading to his imprisonment, in the later years of his life. Unfortunately his only crime, was for believing in his truly miraculous discoveries, for this he would eventually pay the ultimate price, for what he truly believed in, with all his heart. Unfortunately, one of the greatest minds of the twentieth century, would spend the last days of his life, in a prison environment. Fortunately his work, has now been re - researched, by many of the modern day scientific community, which has now led to a full vindication of his life's work, and scientific findings, being correct. Many of his early experiments, have now been repeated, and also validate. This as been done, using more modern day technology, and equipment. These new experiment's, have been able to go much further, being able to look much deeper, into this truly fascinating subject. This as brought us, ever closer, to the secrets of life itself, thank you Dr Wilhelm Reich, for your outstanding contribution, to life on this planet. I started to look deeper into orgone energy, and to try and find out the modern day prospective on this valuable, and fascinating subject. What i found, at this time, truly startled, and also amazed me, many people, from all over the planet, were constructing their own orgone energy devices, based on the many years of studies, that was done by Dr Wilhelm Reich. These devices came in all shapes, and sizes, and seemed to be designed for what ever the purpose, the designer picked for that particular device, at that time. These truly magical orgone energy devices, were mostly built using the original instructions, and plans that Dr Wilhelm Reich had left, has a gift to our world. The many different designs, and uses for these many orgone energy devices, begun to spring up from all area's of the planet, this was again, a magnificent statement, to the true brilliance of the human imagination. Most of the orgone energy gathering devices, which circulated the internet, were only small in their size, but this in no way affected their strength, in fact they were extremely powerful for their small size. These many different energy devices, were designed and made, to gather, and store up the orgone energy, from the invisible field of energy, that Wilhelm Reich had discovered sum sixty years before. The most amazing effect of these devices, was not only their capacity to store, and attract orgone energy from the invisible energy field, but also their capacity to amplify the effect, of the orgone energy from the field. Once it was inside the device, the orgone energy was then stored, and could be used for many different purposes. But one use, caught my eye immediately, it was the effect the energy field had on the human body. The orgone energy had qualities of healing the human body, revitalizing and also restoring the human body, with its life force energy. I was again drawn to healing, on my life'e journey, even if it was indirectly. I seemed to be on a path towards healing, and there seemed to be no turning away from my destiny. I was again beginning to feel new excitement in my life, at last my life, was seeming to make sense to me, i was at last finding my true purpose for being here on this planet. This feeling was more than happiness, it also seemed like a great relief, that i had finally found my true calling in this life time. I was truly grateful with all my heart, knowing that many people on this planet today, may never even get to this point, in their own life's journey, some how, missing out, on all that they were born for, in this amazing world, this time around. The next thing i wanted to do, was get my hands, on one of these orgone energy devices, and discover for my self, their true healing powers. There were many people selling these orgone energy devices, all over the internet, including many on eBay, and many other different sites, from all around the world. I knew that i needed to be extremely careful, in picking the person who i would eventually purchase my orgone energy device's from. There seemed to be many stories all over the internet, claiming that many people, were not using the right materials, and were also not following the original instruction, that Dr Wilhelm Reich had given to humanity, many years before. This at first, seemed like quite a challenge to me, their was such a large number of people selling these devices, and of course they all claimed to have the best devices on the internet, but how would i know, how would i choose the right person, to buy from. At this point, i again ask for inner guidance, and late one night while looking on eBay, for orgone energy devices, one of the sellers name's, stood out to me, and again it seemed to have glowing properties, around it. The name was suli, and straight away, that name had a great meaning to me, and i instantly knew, that this was the person, i would buy my orgone energy devices from. I was extremely excited, i knew again that my request for help, had been answered, and it was also in a way, that i could not have mistaken. Suli was not a popular name, and for that person, also to be selling orgone energy devices wow!!!!, what can i say. I immediately contacted suli for some information, on the devices, that i had finally chosen from his eBay shop. Unbelievably the two devices that immediately stood out to me, were pyramid in shape, more coincidences, and pointers, seemed to be guiding me. Suli explained in a email, that the devices would take two weeks to construct, explaining they were only built to order, and they were also built with special care, and commitment, in their construction. I was like a child at Christmas, waiting for his present's, the wait was agonizing for me, the excitement was overflowing out of me, like a fountain of joy. The day eventually arrived, i was working away at work, when i spotted the post office van, as it pulled up outside my works entrance. This was a regular appearance of the post van, we were always getting post on a daily basis. But i knew, at that moment, that this was the long awaited arrival of my orgone energy devices. I was extremely excited at their arrival, and i couldn't wait to test them out for myself, the anticipation engulfed my entire being. I eventually ordered four orgone energy devices, all shaped in the style of a pyramid, each displaying a different colour, the colour defining their use, and purpose. The colours i picked were, two black, with real gold shavings at the tip of the pyramid, a red pyramid, and also a green pyramid. The orgone energy devices, came with extensive paper work, and suggested instructions for their proper use. When i eventually opened the packages containing my new orgone energy devices, i was still at my works. I felt that i couldn't have waited until i was at home, the suspense was overwhelming to say the least. I found a quite spot in my office, and closed the door, letting my work colleagues know, i couldn't be disturbed for a few minutes or so. When i picked up one of the orgone energy devices, out of the packaging, and held it in my hand, i could immediately feel the device emitting energy, what i mean by that, i could feel my hands tingling. I also got, what i call a magnetic feeling, like when you try to push two magnets together, and they repel themselves, the power of these little devices was astonishing. At first i thought i must be imagining it, but i also got one of my employees, to hold it in his hands, and he immediately said his hands was also tingling, Wow!!. I was totally blown away, by their interactions with the human body, i know i had read up on many of their effects on the human body, but feeling it for myself was amazing, and also quite gratifying in a way. I couldn't wait to finish work, and get home to study the paper work, that had come with these special energy devices. I then placed them in my bag, for safe keeping, till it was time for me to go home. When i arrived home, i didn't even want my tea, i explained to Wendy, that i just wanted to get bathed, and study my new orgone energy devices. Wendy just laughed, and said i was mad, but i didn't really care at the time, and i knew she didn't really mean it. Once i was clean and bathed, i went in to my study, and began to read the paper work, that accompanied the energy devices. I also held the energy devices while reading the paper work, i was still feeling there powerful effects on my body. At first the energy devices, started to make me feel a little dizzy, and light headed, but i knew this was only a temporary feeling, and i had already read about these sensations. This dizzy feeling, and light headiness, was the surge of life force energy, entering the body, and removing any energy blockages, that may be present in the body. After five or ten minutes, the feeling began to subside, and a feeling of calm and comfort, engulfed my entire being. After reading about the many uses of these amazing orgone energy devices, i began to use these them while i was meditating, holding the devices in one of my hands. I began to notice their very strong effects immediately, it seemed to enhance the deepness of my meditation, and at first, it even made the room spin, sending me into, a trance like state of mind. I have got to be entirely honest here, these new feelings that i was getting, from my new orgone energy devices, was taking me quite some time to get comfortable with them. After three, or four meditation sessions using the devices, the effects started to settle down, and i felt i could control the new sensations a lot more. The other amazing affect, that i found the devices had, when i placed them in key areas around my house, was a feeling of new energy. The devices started to affect my whole family, including my two children, Danielle, and Kyle, and also my wife Wendy. I don't think my family even noticed this for themselves at first, but they all seemed to be happier within themselves, and life in generally. This new affect started to snowball, in the weeks that followed, even my children and wife, also started to notice, that they were feeling different, and happier. I tried to explain it was the orgone energy devices, causing their new found feelings, and the extra energy they had, but again only my son Kyle, wanted to believe me. But i didn't mind, as long as i could see the effects for myself, and the effects were truly amazing. I would greatly encourage every reader of this book to buy one or more, of these orgone energy devices, and try it for yourselves. At this point, i now believe the blue aura, which i have now been seeing around living, and also non living things, in the last few months of my life's journey, is the orgone energy which Dr Wilhelm Reich discovered, and also researched for most of his life. I started to fully accept that i was seeing this energy field, i am starting to believe this may be connected in some way, to my life purpose of healing. I can now sense a big change coming for me in my life, but i am not afraid of it, i have complete faith in myself, and God. I feel my heart is opening wide, to the many new adventures, that i now see laid out before me. I can almost feel the pull of the mysterious, and magical adventures that lie in front of me, taking my life in all new directions, with a sense of great new discoveries ahead of me. Taking me to many new, and different places i could only of dreamed about. In the days, and weeks that followed, my new orgone energy devices, started to intensify the effects, of the strange mist like phenomenon, which i mentioned in early chapters, while in deep meditation. It was now starting to become more pronounced, the misty like fog, seemed to be getting much denser, i am now sure that the mist like fog, has intelligence controlling it some how. I was starting to interact, and possibly communicate with it, in some way, it was now starting to definitely follow my hand movements, and even started to swirl around my face, time, and time again. At times, i thought i could physically feel it brush past my skin, i would get a sort of tingling sensation on my skin, when the mist seemed to touch me. It was like the hairs on my whole body, would stand on end. These newer, and more intense sensations, have only just started to happen in the last few meditation sessions, they have been so strong, and visual at times, i have been quite startled by them. The swirling mist seems to be intensifying by the day, and at one stage a couple of nights ago, my whole body, felt as though, it was being lifted off the the couch, where i was lay. The feeling was very strange indeed, my whole body felt as though it had been lifted, possibly by the mist like substance. At that point i got a shiver through my whole body, i have to be honest here, i immediately stopped the meditation session, in a bit of a panic. I wasn't really sure what had just happened to me, and i was a bit taken back by it all. But deep down, i was sure that no harm would have come to me. Later i came to realize that i was hitting another deeper level of meditation, that to date, i hadn't experienced in any of my past meditation sessions. I still had no explanation for this strange mist like substance, but over the last few days, i have manage to read a few internet stories regarding the phenomena. There seems to be two camps on this matter, and they both have their own explanations regarding it. One camp saying it is our own bodies aura field, the other camp saying, it's a inter dimensional door way of some kind. At this point, i am not very sure, what to make of both of these explanations, but both camps seem to agree on one fact, that this mist like substances, has some sort of intelligence to it, just like, i thought it had, and it definitely interacts with you in different ways. These short internet stories only confirmed what i already knew, but i also found great comfort in all of them, knowing i wasn't the only one, to experience these strange enigmas. I didn't feel so alone anymore. At this point of my life's journey, these new findings, which i seemed to be coming across on a daily basis, were getting quite difficult to take in, and also to deal with, on my own. Here i was, only a year a so before, living a normal existence, with a normal family life, but then i was thrust into a totally new world, a world of endless possibilities, full of hidden secrets, and mystery. A new world, taking me on new adventures, i could only ever of dreamed about. This is what i have always dreamed of, the magic of life, the one i knew was there all the time, waiting for me to discover it. I was now, well on my way to living the life, i was always meant to live. My old way of thinking, and living seemed to be fading away from my mind, at break neck speed, the world i used to live in, now seems like a distant illusion to me. The things i have experienced in my life, over last eighteen months are truly stranger than words can express. The fact, i feel that i cannot tell anyone about them at this point, saddens me greatly. But i truly hope with all my heart, that the publication of this book, will bring this knowledge, and information to a vast audience, all around the world. I really long to tell all of my family members, but i feel afraid of their reactions to these many new, and strange parts of my expanding world. I continue to share these new experiences with my beautiful young son Kyle, his love and understanding are truly amazing, and inspirational to me. In time i also hope my amazing wife Wendy, and my beautiful daughter Danielle, will truly see what i can now see, giving life a chance to show them, what it is beginning to show me, opening up their hearts and minds, to the true wonders of this magical life. But at this moment in time, i treat these difference's, in me, and my families lives, as a great advantage, i believe this creates a good balance in my life, and also there's too. This balance, i believe, is what makes our lives so special here on planet earth, we all need different aspects of life, a bit of both sides, yin, and yang, if you like. I believe these difference's in our lives, is what make us so special, has human being's, we all make our own contributions to this life, making it the amazing thing it is today.

CHAPTER 21

Pineal Gland

I received another sign today, concerning my destiny, of becoming a healer of some kind. The continuing arrival of more pointers, and signs in my daily life, seemed to be leading me further along the road, of my true destiny. I was doing a reading with my new, and trusted animal cards, by Steven D. Farmer PhD, which i have been using a lot lately. The many answers i have been getting from the cards of late, seemed to be one hundred percent accurate in their answers, to every area of my life. The cards always seemed to know what was going on, at that time in my life, its was amazing, and quite helpful, to say the least. I now knew with a sense of trust, that when i would ask a question of my oracle cards, regarding different areas of my life, i knew the answer given, would always be the best for everybody concerned. I would sit down with my oracle cards in my hands, stating my intention inside my mind only, asking the cards, for their help, and direction in my life. By this point, i had already discovered a new technique, for receiving my answer from my oracle cards. I would spread out the deck, face down, and with the same thought intention in my mind, begin to scan my hands over the oracle cards. Has my hands moved over the cards, one by one, i knew when i had come across the card for my answer, i would begin to feel a tingling sensation within the centre of my hand. This was first time, that i had really asked the cards for direction in my life, but when i picked up the card that night for my answer, it sent shivers all the way down my entire spine, the card i turned over was the healing card. I now feel that it is my density, to heal and help people in some way, what type of healing, i am still not sure. From my research, i know that there are many different types of healing, from physical healing, emotional healing, and many other's, which one is for me, i am still unsure at this point in my life's journey. I feel when i am ready, i will be shown the way, but i now feel within my entire being, that i am destined to heal. Something else, i have begun to notice lately, a lot of people who are coming into my life, through my general home life, and also my work place, all seem to have some sort of bodily illness, from mild to life threatening. The strange part is, without me even asking them anything about their health or personal circumstances, they seem compelled to tell me all about their illnesses, even though i have not consciously enquired about it in any way. I now feel this is some sort of calling for me, or maybe i am being told about their illnesses for other reasons, i do not yet fully understand. I have got to be honest, at this part of my life's journey, i don't feel as though i have any special healing powers, and i wouldn't even know how to go about the healing, of any another persons body. But i do feel, and sense that these are messages for me, a sort of direction for me to follow, as part of my life's path here on this planet. Yesterday day in work, i had a strange experience, one of our regular customers, who had been coming the garage for many years to have his car repaired, out of the blue, and quite unexpected, told me that his youngest son had tragically died two years earlier. I was quite shocked by this, he had never mentioned this before to anyone in the garage, we then talked about his son, for next twenty minutes or so. I could see in his eyes, that it was still very painful, and upsetting for him to talk about his sons death. But i feel that this man needed to talk about his sons tragic death, and i felt truly honored, that he trusted me to listen to him. At first i wasn't quite sure what to say to him, but from somewhere inside me, words seemed to flow out of me, that i wouldn't usually of said to anybody. I still don't no where i found the comforting words from till this day, but i am so glad that i did, the words seemed to comfort him in a way, that i could visually see it on his face, he seemed very relieved, just to talk about it, with me. I remembered him, thanking me for listening, saying phil you just seem to be saying all the right things to me, after he left, i got a nice feeling inside myself, it felt like a sense of inner calmness, and i was truly glad that i also give this man a sense of peace too. I feel something is very close, i feel it happening, from within me, even though this change has been happening for the best part of twenty four months, i feel has though it is speeding up, and gaining momentum inside of me. The people close to me, and around me on a daily basis, also seem to be picking up on it to. I have also noticed some sort of heightened perception, it started by what i can only refer to has, speaking whats on peoples minds. By this i mean, i would be having a conversation with a friend, or complete stranger, then i would seem to bring up a subject out of the blue in the conversation, and the person i would be talking to, would say thats very strange, i was just about to say the same thing. I know things like this can happen, from time to time, but lately with me, its happening nearly all of the time. There are many other strange things, that seem to be happening lately, i would be thinking of a person, it could be anyone, that just seemed to pop into my mind, and minutes later, i would get a call from that same person, or they would turn up at my work or home, or i would even bump into them, while i was out, and about. This happened twice at work yesterday, i was thinking of ringing a company who owed us some outstanding money, minutes later, they called to pay their bill, which was a very nice surprise, to say the least. This was not the first time, it seems lately everything i am giving a sustained thought to, seems to happen in my life, or some sort of equivalent event. These many strange events seemed to have happened, since adding, the pineal gland, or third eye exercise into my meditations. This involves visualizing the opening up of the third eye, and letting in pure white light, then imagining your self looking through the third eye, which is in the middle of the forehead. The pineal gland has long been associated with extra sensory perception. All of the ancient cultures from around the world, like the Egyptians, knew this thousands of years ago, this was so exciting for me, because i had only been incorporating this into my mediations for just a few weeks, and i could definitely notice some new, and amazing changes within my life, and also my extra sensory abilities. The pineal gland is truly fascinating, it is only the size of a grain of rice, and it lies at the base of the skull. It has been mentioned by many of the worlds ancient culture's in our planets history, from all around the globe. Thousands of years ago, they truly knew the importance of this little gland, at the base of our skulls, using it to help them discover, and also understand many of life's greatest mysteries. Its said to be the eye of the soul, you can see many monuments all over the ancient, and modern world today, depicting the shape of the pine cone, which is said to bear a great resemblance to the pineal gland. I recommend that everybody reading this book now, researches this little gland for themselves, i feel that its holds great discoveries for all our lives. Modern science, has now discovered that the cells of the pineal gland, resemble the retinal cone cells, in the human eyes. We are only now beginning to discover, and uncover the many mysteries, contained within our own human bodies, and mind. I feel that our future's truly hold, untold treasure's, and riches, just around the corner, awaiting our discovery.

CHAPTER 22

Digging Deeper

Over the next few weeks, my mind seemed to be thinking of Jake a lot, this wasn't a bad thing, the memories i was recalling, were of the best times i had with him. I felt that i was letting myself know, just how much Jake had really supported me, through a large part of my life, here on this planet. I didn't quite know why, but i seemed to be getting the feeling, that Jake had been much more than just a pet, and great friend to me, in this life time. I now believe jake was watching over me in some way, i feel he was my earthly guardian, and guide to get me to this point in my life. I also strongly believe, Jake death marked a definite junction in my life. Jakes death seemed to coincide exactly, with the starting of my new life's journey, along a different path, than the one i had been living for so long, here on this planet. When i now think back to the point of Jake's death, even though Jake was a dog, i still feel that we also communicated, on some sort of subconscious level, almost letting me know, that it was his time to go, and i must move forward in my life, on my own, without his help. It was as though he already knew, he had done everything he could for me in this life, and it was time for me to go it alone. I now believe this very strongly, as strange as this may sound to some people, especially if you have never owned a dog, or a pet of any kind. But i believe that this connection is the same connection, and bond, that we make with our families, and also our friends in this life. Once we love anything with all our heart, the connection to that being is so strong, it is never lost, it remains with you forever. From my own personal experience, of having children, and also having a family dog, of seventeen years, the connection to Jake was also very strong, and the upset of letting him go, was truly heart wrenching to say the least. When you have shared a large part of your life, with anyone, human being, or animal, the connection, i believe will never fully be lost. Even now, at this point, i still feel Jake's presents very strongly, somewhere in side my own being. I sometimes think i can actually see him, or just catch little glimpses of him passing the corner of my vision, but i could never be certain, but it still feels nice inside, just thinking he is still round and about. But there comes a time in life, when we all must partial separate, from our love one's, or we may never move on, and learn to find our own path in this life. When i now think back, Jake was always there for me, even down to letting me know, if certain people in my life, were the right choice for me. I had a few, not so good friends over the years, and Jake always seemed to take a instant dislike to every one of them, if only i had listened to him at that time, it would have saved me lot's of heart ache. He always seemed to lift me up, just at the right times in my life, bringing me back from the brink of disaster, in some way or other. He seemed on many occasions to reflect back to me the way i was acting, and feeling at that point in time, trying to show me, how bad i was acting. Sometimes i would notice, and take action, other times, i am afraid i didn't listen at all. I felt he was a mirror reflection of me, reflecting many pieces of my life, and details back to me. Lately i have started to get restless, and distant at work, and i have been slowly loosing interest in my current work career, and environment. Don't get me wrong, i still did my work to the best of my abilities, and i always will, but i seemed to becoming more, and more dissatisfied with my current work, and career choice. I always thought this was the career for me, but now i am not so sure, i feel very guilty about these new thoughts in my mind, i have my own business, it has given me, and my family, a wonderful life, but i feel there is a void inside my heart, and i feel that this profession, and path, is not filling that void. I knew deep down that this profession was not the one for me, i was getting to the point of feeling quite unhappy, and depressed at times. Even though i had discovered these amazing new secret's about life, i still felt quite trapped by these new feelings, and emotions about not knowing what to do, about my current career path. I felt i couldn't talk to anybody, and when i did try, all i got was your being silly, you have a great job, and also a great career, many people are not so lucky in their life, so be grateful, and get on with it. I knew this to be true, but i just could not help how i felt at this point in time, it was strange, i seemed to be very happy one day, and then down a for a few days, my feelings were all over the place. I was getting a feeling, deep within my heart, that this was only ever a temporary, or stepping stone career for me. When i now think back, i never really wanted to join the family business, but because of circumstances at the time of me leaving school, i truly thought they were out of my control. I also felt as though i had no other options open to me, at that time. I feel now, i have always known that this career was never the one for me, a strange feeling of knowing deep within myself. I feel that it has never really given me that spark, or filled me with a sense of achievement or mystery, which i now feel, i have always been looking for in my life. I am finding it quite hard to cope with many of these new emotions, and feelings, after all this is a family run business, and it has given me, and my family, the many things, i now have in my life, including financial security, which i am truly grateful for in every way. Many people around this planet, would be truly happy with what i have in my life, but i now feel inside of myself, this is not the right path for me, and i am starting to feel myself being pulled slowly away from this past life. But i can't help but feel anxious because of the loyalties to my family members, as well as the many financial implications of leaving this family business. This was giving me a horrible feeling of helplessness inside of myself, i just had a feeling inside me, that i could be of more help to people, if i wasn't trapped, in this career path. At this point in my life's journey, i knew i had to make some tough choices, and also sacrifices in my current life, before i could move on to a new path of discovery, and enlightenment. I seemed to hit a low point around this time, i was being torn between this new amazing life, i had only just discovered, and also never new existed before this point. I could still feel the chains from my old way of life, firmly holding me down, and i could not find a way to break free of them. These emotionally charged feelings were starting to drain me, and was also leaving me in a sort of depression state of mind. Weeks later, i hit new feelings of even wishing i didn't know about all of these new discoveries, and knowledge in my life, i just felt i wanted to go back to my old life, not knowing anything about these new discoveries. Then i knew at that point, once you go down this new road, and find these new life changing discoveries, which i had been asking for in my life, for so long, i knew then in my heart, that there was definitely no going back to my old way of living my life. A day or so later, these feelings seemed to leave me, and subside, and i instantly felt much better, and relieved inside of myself. I started to have more dreams, these dreams were very vivid, and also very detailed, they showed me path's of health, and prosperity, they were giving me new hope in my life's journey, and also new amounts of much needed energy. I then knew, what i needed to do, i had dreams, with visions if you like, i felt i knew how to make my desires, and dreams a physical reality in my life. And once i did, i would share this amazing knowledge with every other person on this planet today. Straight away after using these new visions, and feelings, i started to mix them with my new understanding of this mysterious life. I immediately started to see new, and amazing developments in my family run business, which i felt would change all of our lives, for the better. At this point i felt a inner calm come over my entire being, i knew, and also sensed that i was being watched over, by an unseen force, that was all around me. My family and i were about to embark on new business ventures around the world, this was a dream come true for me and my family, and up until this point in our lives, we could have never imagined that we would be traveling around the world, doing business in other foreign countries, this was me living my actual dreams. We were all truly grateful for this new direction in our lives, it gave us all a new sense of excitement, and new found vigor in our lives. I knew these newly found circumstances in our lives, were divinely given, and also guided. Even though my brother, and father were also taken back, by this new direction that our lives were heading down, they didn't agree with my explanation for our new found prosperity. But i didn't seem to care, i just knew that all our lives, were on a great journey of mystery, and new discoveries. I now know that when you put your complete faith in God, even when you cannot see the bigger invisible picture of our life's path, the fact remains that all our earthly lives are being guided in some way, we just have to trust in this almighty power, which seems to know what is best for us in this life. I now believe that this invisible force truly guides, every aspect of our earthly lives, and also continues to guide us into the next life, beyond this earthly realm. I now believe that when i hit my low points, in my life's journey, i felt a great feeling of helplessness inside myself, through what seemed at the time, to be almost impossible circumstances, turned into something totally unexpected, leading me, and my family into new, and exciting destines, along our life's path's, which we could of only dreamed about doing, a year or so before. We could have never predicted the many strange set of circumstances, which led us to our new business adventures, i feel i could write many more books, just on these many strange, and truly mysterious set of events leading to this new path in our lives, and maybe one day, i just might do that, who knows, life is truly magical, in ever way. These new business ventures, have led me, and my family, to discover an amazing new country called Dubai. This truly breath taking country, immediately captured all of our hearts, and we all totally fell in love with it. I was truly amazed by this great islamic nation, and their truly visionary way of thinking, in many area's of human progression in life. We all look forward to a future of regular visit's to this magical land. I feel now at this stage of my life's journey, i have learned a very valuable lesson, when things seem to be going off course in your life, and your life may look like a disaster area, you must continue to keep complete faith, that the outcome will turn out, to be the best for all concerned. This act of believing in the unseen, will begin to transform your life, and give you the power, to live the life of your wildest dreams. We must learn to turn around, many of life's negative, and stressful situations. I believe we must learn to adapt our way of thinking, and begin acting differently, to many of our daily stressful situations in life. Instead of the reaction of panic, and the endless fighting with life's negative circumstances, we must begin to see these events as lesson's, that we have chosen for ourselves, this time around, on our life's journey, here on this planet. This is where many people in their lives, seemed to get swamped down, and end up turning away from their true life's purpose, and begin to loose sight of their true dreams, ending up never for fulfilling their true hearts desires, leaving a large void within their lives. I now believe, from many of my own personal experiences, that many of life's negatives situations, may not turn out to be, so negative at all, we as human beings, only perceive them, as being negative, because we cannot see the greater, unseen plan of our lives. I truly hope this gives the reader a prospective in their own lives, what once seemed like a disaster in my life, has led me to a new, and exciting life, in many areas, from health, happiness, and also prosperity, this list is truly endless. I have now also been given the amazing gift, of being able to explore more of this truly amazing planet, which i have always wanted to do, deep down. I feel i need to mention two people here, one is Mr Khan, and the other is Mr Sabih, i cannot thank these two amazing people enough, for everything they have done for me, and my family, going far beyond their professional duties, to me, and also my family, god bless them both, i love them dearly with all my heart, thank you.

CHAPTER 23

Manifestation Revisited

This chapter i have decided to call manifestation revisited. At this stage of my life's journey, i have come to a realization, that if you truly want something with all your heart, and it is for the greater good of all concerned, you really can have it. This is where i started to really take a look a certain area's of my life, and then i said to myself, i really want to change this part of my life. If you do this for yourself, and really take the time to feel with your heart, you will begin to see, all the areas's of your own life, that you are not truly happy with, and you would like to turn them completely around. I have got to be honest here, even though the greater parts of my life's journey so far, have been what i class as being spiritually awakened, to the invisible, and magical world, that surrounds us all. I am still like most people on this planet, and i still want the many so called material things in life, financial freedom, the big house, the fast cars, and i always had a dream of winning the lottery, and maybe a few other little things as well, but i will try to keep the list as short a possible here. I would also like to stress an important point here, i have not come across any information, in any part of my life's journey, through any of my readings, or through any other material that i have come across, or have i ever felt inside myself, that wanting more prosperity, or more of the many material things that life has to offer us, is bad in anyway. In fact, i have come to understanding, that totally the opposite seems to be true. If you yourself are truly wealthy, you then have the chance to share your wealth for the greater good, and help as many people as possible with it. Wealth gives you the chance to return something back, to the less fortunate people of this planet. I also feel, that if you are finically secure yourself, it can truly make your life here on this planet, a whole lot easier, in-turn allowing your life to become much happier, and worry-free. Please don't misunderstand me here, and get me totally wrong, wealth if handled wrongly, can just as easy destroy lives, it goes back to the issues that i have mentioned before, there must be balance in every area of your life, including wealth. The choice, is totally your own, with great wealth, i believe comes great responsibility. So i began to think to myself, how could i change my current life circumstances, with my new amazing knowledge, of how life really works. Even though, at this point in my life, i felt quite content in most areas of my life, but that said, even with my new family business successes, i still felt that i was doing a job, that i knew, my heart was not in, and i felt, it was not truly part of my true life's purpose here on this planet. At this point, i again knew inside myself, that if you are totally off course, from what you came here on earth to do this time around, you would not be able to find true happiness in your life time. I then started to think back, to when i started my life's journey of new discoveries, i began to remember some of my amazing early successes, that i had, with the many items, that i had already manifested into my life, with this great mysterious, and magical knowledge, that i had been truly blessed with. In my minds eye, i then started to picture the many events, and the extraordinary circumstances, that i had already drawn into every area of my life, using this powerful, and secret information. I then started to plan for something, much bigger, i wanted to start with my eyes, even though i still had 20/20 vision in both eyes, my eye sight sharpness was slowly starting to leave me. This can be quite upsetting for anybody, to experience any sort of deterioration in their vision, it can be very traumatic to say the least. I wanted to use, my new found knowledge, to help save, and turn around my vision's deterioration, stoping my eyes from deteriorating any further, and getting to the stage of needing glasses. This is not a criticism of people who wear glasses, i know many people around the planet, use glasses on a daily basis, my own mother uses them, but she would also prefer not to, if she had the choice. This is just my own personal preference, and a dislike of using glasses, i also know that many people around the world, may like wearing their glasses, and that's fine too. We all have our own choices, dislike's, and like's, that's why i love this life. I have tried numerous ways to keep my eye sight from deteriorating, i have purchased eye exercise machines, from the internet, and pinhole glasses, which i also bought from the internet. These devices, did give me some slight improvements in my vision, but i needed to use them on a daily basis, and it was also a continuous requirement, to keep their effects going. But after a while, i am just like every body else's, i seemed to get bored of using them, i was looking for a more permanent solution to my eye problems. The next root i went down, was laser eye surgery, even though laser eye surgery has been about for the last fifteen years, it is only fairly recently, that it has been widely available, and affordable to the general public. After applying for the first time, to one of the well known laser eye surgery company's, they told me because my eyes were still able to achieve 20/20 on the vision charts, they could not see any reason, for me to have laser eye surgery at this time. I tried to explain to them, that my eyes were not as sharp as they used to be, but they insisted, saying it was not worth taking the risk, for such a slight improvement in my vision. If your anything like me, i think my eyes are the most precious things in our bodies, and even the slightest risk of complications, was definitely a no, no for me. This is where i would try to use my new found knowledge, to help me manifest a solution to this health problem. I don't know, what i was expecting to happen. In a way, i was thinking along the lines, of a instant miracle cure, maybe i would wake up one morning, with perfect vision, how great would that be. After applying my new found knowledge to this health problem, for a few weeks, nothing seemed to happen, then about three weeks later while i was downloading my daily emails at work, there in my inbox was a promotional email, from one of the larger laser eye surgery companies. There was a large font heading, with a message about a new laser device, that was now making it possible to treat people, who was not suitable for laser eye surgery, with the older laser devices. It seemed it was now possible to treat people with only slight deterioration in their vision, which was the exact condition, i felt i had with my eyes. I then felt, and knew this was my chance, and the universe had answered my hearts wishes, with an unusual set of circumstances. After booking a appointment for two weeks later, i was eventually accessed, by a pre laser eye surgery doctor, the doctor tested my eye's, and i was still showing 20/20 vision on the eye chart test's. But i explained that the sharpness had gone from my vision. She then reassured me, that with this new advanced laser, they would be able to remove the slightest imperfections from my eye's, and give me back, crystal clear vision again. I was extremely excited by our conversation, i immediately booked an appointment to have my laser eye surgery treatment, some two weeks later. Two weeks later, i arrived at the laser eye surgery clinic, i was very nervous indeed, there was quite a few people there, also waiting to have their laser eye surgery. I decided to strike up a conversation with them, i think i was just trying to calm my own nerves, before the imminent laser eye surgery. After having two, or three different conversations with the waiting people, i think it calmed all of our nerves. I had been waiting in the surgery area, for some thirty minutes or so, i was then called for my pre surgery discussion, with the laser eye surgeon, who would be doing my surgery. I was told it would be a different surgeon, than the one who did my consultation, some weeks before. To my great surprise, the pre-surgery discussion room, was just like a normal office room, with a chair in the corner of the room, for me to sit on. As i sat down in the chair, i could see the nurse, and also the laser eye surgeon, across the other side of the room. They were both reading through a folder of documents, i immediately felt a sense of unease in the room, between the surgeon, and the nurse. The laser eye surgeon, then turned, and looked across at me, he then ask me why i wanted to have the laser eye surgery, when my vision was still achieving 20/20 on the vision chart. I explained to him, like i had done some weeks before to the other eye doctor, that my vision, was not as sharp has it used to be. He immediately started to explain that my vision was still changing, and he felt that there were still some slight risk's in doing the laser eye surgery at this time. He basically said that the final decision, had to be made by me, but he was still willing to carry on with the laser eye surgery, if i wanted to go ahead with it. But he also made it pretty clear to me, that his professional recommendation, was not to have the laser eye surgery done, at this point in time. As i sat there in the pre-surgery room, surrounded by three strangers, i began to fill up, with a fountain of different emotions, i knew, i only had a few minutes to make a decision, on what i felt was a monumental, and truly life changing one. This was a decision, on the future of my valuable vision, which i cared so passionately about. I did have a feeling inside myself, telling me everything would be ok, this was God giving me my chance, to have perfect vision back, in my life, and this is what i had been asking for, and i should keep the faith, and stick with it. But i just panicked, and said no to the laser eye surgery. I said that i will take your professional advice, and not have the surgery done, at this point in time. At that point, i felt that my new found faith, had let me down, right at the last minute, i cannot tell you how disappointed i felt within myself, at that point. I couldn't stop thinking, this was God giving me my wish, that i myself, had ask for, and i had just walked away from it. I felt like a complete, and ungrateful fool, at this point. I wasn't to sure, if i was more disappointed with letting my self down, or more with letting God down. I felt i was shown the way, and my faith let me down right at the last hurdle. But what i now know, and believe to be the truth, this whole episode, of my laser eye surgery disappointment, was just another test in my life's journey, that i needed to go through at this point in time. I also believe that i have come out of this negative situation, with a very positive outcome. I feel a more stronger, and better person, and i have definitely acquired more faith than ever before. From that point on, i made a promise to myself, that this would never happen again. What seemed at first to be a defeat, later on, turned out to be a great triumph, and a invaluable lesson, which i felt i needed to go through, to progress to the next level of understanding of how God really works. The most amazing part of this lesson was weeks later, when my vision, out of the blue seemed to be getting better, for no apparent reason. I hadn't been doing any new eye exercises, or anything new at all, in fact i had totally stop thinking about my vision problem all together. I just started to notice things becoming much clearer, road signs, car no plates, all seemed much sharper, also my night vision seemed to start improving, this was the miracle i had been looking for. Even though my eyes were still not perfect, they were getting better, and better by the day. What this valuable lesson seemed to teach me, was when things don't always go the way you want them to, it does't mean that its going to turn out to be a bad thing. There is always something much better, just around the corner, waiting for you. As human beings, we always seem to miss the bigger unseen picture. I believe its just a matter of having complete faith, in the unseen world, thats surrounds us. It was definitely a case of the genie in a lamp, just ask for what you want, truly believe it with all of your heart, matched with your minds thoughts, and you can truly have anything you desire in this life. After this enlightening episode, i started thinking even bigger thoughts, i have always wanted to win the lottery, just like every other person around the planet, especially the euro millions jackpot. It wasn't just for the money, it was what the money was able to give you, the freedom to live the life of your dreams, and not be chained, and tied to our daily life routines, the nine till five jobs etc. So i decided from this point, to make this my next goal, and i really went for it, i started to put pictures up everywhere at work, on my iPhone, iPad, my computer screen savers, of myself holding the winning euro millions mega jackpot cheque in my hands. It was very easy to do, anybody can do it, with one of the many photo editing software packages, available today. I even began to put the winning amount on the cheque which was £96,00,497,10. I had already been having, very vivid dreams, of winning the euro millions jackpot, and this amount was on the cheque in my very vivd dreams. I also noticed that this amount, had embedded in it, my life's path number, along with a few other of my important numerology numbers, regarding my life. The images that i edited with the photo editing software, were all very convincing, many people would see them on my office wall at work, and say, have you really won the lottery, they really did look, very realistic. I also used my new photo editing skills, to add myself to pictures of cars i wanted to have, i also added myself to the dream house i wanted to live in. I started to put these pictures up in every single place, so i would begin to see them every single day of my life. My workplace started to fill up with them, my home also started to fill up with them, i wanted to engrain these images into my consciousness, and also my subconsciousness mind, until the point came, when they actually seemed to become part, of my every day physical reality. I tried to be as discreet as possible at first, but eventually every body started to notice the images. To many people, it seemed like very strange behavior indeed. But i just shrugged, and laughed it off, not really giving them the answers they were looking for. Eventually after a few months, people just seemed to ignore it, and began to take much less notice, unless they had not seen some of the edited images before. I also started to visit car showrooms, and sit in my dream car, enquiring about purchasing it, really starting to enforce the reality of my dreams on to my waking self, living the dream if you like. The car i dreamed of having, was the amazing Audi R8, Wow!! what a car. I searched for my dream house, on the many internet selling sites, i found a very special one, i immediately fell in love with it. I would sometimes drive past it at the weekends, imagining myself owning it. I know to some people, this will seem very strange, and extreme to point of obsessive, and you may even think i'm just plain weird, but what i began to notice, was the appearance of strange little signs, and messages, that seemed to be happening all around me. In the months that followed, these many signs, and messages seemed to intensifying themselves, they were very sutle indeed at first, and if you wasn't paying very close attention, you would definitely miss them. At first it would be simple things, like a customer would turn up at work, and while in conversation, they would bring up in the conversation, the area, where the dream house i wanted to buy was located. Other days, when i was in a conversation with some one, out of the blue, they would mention the lottery to me. At first i just put these down to normal every day coincidences. But as time progressed, it was getting much more than just a normal set of coincidences. I really started to take notice, when my friend of some twenty years, or so, came into the garage one evening, and while in a normal conversation with him, somehow, and i am still not sure how it seemed to come about, but he had been working right next to the house, i had picked of the internet, some months before. It turned out that he was working on the road, exactly where my dream house was situated, when i mentioned the house to him, he instantly knew, which one i was referring to. He had also been working there for three years, but he had never mentioned this to me, before now. The lottery again, started to come up in many of my daily conversations, with my work colleagues, and also with the many customers, that i would encounter through my work day. It didn't stop there either, it seemed like i was being bombarded from all area's, regarding anything to do with the lottery. This all seemed to coincide, with my all out manifestation project, of winning the lottery jackpot. As the weeks went by, early one morning i got a telephone call, off one of my closest friends, telling me another close friend, had just won a large amount on the euro millions. I was truly excited for him, after speaking to him in person, at a later date, he had won a substantial amount of money, but he had also only been one number short of winning the jackpot, of ninety six millions pounds. When he told me, i immediately picked up on the jackpot amount, this was the same jackpot amount, i had been dreaming of winning, in my many months of very vivd dreams. I wasn't sure what this meant, but i didn't say anything to him, about my dreams, i was just extremely happy for him, he really did need the money, it would make his life, a whole lot easier, and he was also truly grateful for his win, i could see it in his eyes. I started to see, these many strange coincidences, as little signs from God, that i was on the right track, and i was starting to draw these things towards me. These phenomena, were mentioned in the book The Secret, which i had read, much earlier in my life's journey. It said to look out for these little pointers, and signs, they would let you know, that things were happening for you behind the scenes. In the coming weeks, i would start to see signs on the back of buses, and advert boards saying winner, not like you normally see them, they would seem to stand out brightly, sort of shine, and glow on the edges, just like they had done, early on, in my life's journey. What i also picked up on was when i was happy and feeling in a good positive mood, i noticed the signs more, and more, but if i was in a negative mood or feeling down, the signs seemed to totally vanish, i even noticed that the signs would vanish, when i seemed to be rushing about everywhere. The fact that i was rushing about in my life, seemed to make me miss everything around me, sort of turning myself off from the world, and not communicating with God. I now truly believe that negativity, really does push all good things away from us, and puts you further away from all that you truly want in your life. I believe that these signs, are always there for us all to see in our lives, you just have to open your eyes to see them. As time went on, i would also start seeing the car i wanted, even twice in one day, which is very unusual, because Audi R8's are quite rare in my area, they have a price tag of over £125,000 pounds. This was an extraordinary, and exciting time for me, and i was filled with great desire, and passion for my future. I had been doing my all out manifestation for a month or two, when i was starting to think to myself, how the euro millions was going to get to a jackpot of ninety six million pounds again, when to date, i think this had only happened, a very few times in the euro millions history. I then knew i had made my first big mistake, by doubting god, asking myself how was it possible, i tried to gather my thoughts, and focus myself, it wasn't easy at all. Then on my way to work one morning, i had an email on my iPhone from the lottery, announcing a mega jackpot draw of eighty five million pounds. I knew this wasn't the amount i had dreamed about winning, but i couldn't help thinking, this must somehow be my chance. I tried to stay nice, and calm, and tried not to think about it, but it was impossible, and slowly i could feel the thoughts of, you are never going to win this, its impossible, and as much as i tried, and wanted to keep the faith, my mind was saying no way, and guess what, i didn't win. I think the jackpot eventually climbed to over one hundred million pounds, at this point, i started to feel overwhelmed with disappointment, and i could feel myself pushing my desires further, and further away from myself. This happened again on another occasion when again, the euro millions jackpot climbed close to the amount i was dreaming of winning, but again at the last minute, i started to bring into my mind, many thoughts of doubt, and disappointment. I also started to notice that the lottery dreams, were getting less frequent, and also less vivid in their detail. I have got to be honest, this went on for some twelve to fourteen months, with just the odd signs, and reminders of my lottery dream, house, and car. I still seemed to win small amounts, every week from the lottery, but it was never the amount, i had dreamed of winning. It was hard, but i still kept the faith, and every time i never won the jackpot, it just made me more, and more determined to carry on with my crusade. Then again on this life's journey, i was guided to a new book, by Wallace D Wattles. The books title, was the Science of getting Rich, i have to be honest, i had already heard of this nearly one hundred year old book before, it was the book that inspired Rhonda Byrne, to write the secret, but for some reason or other, i had never studied it till now. But when i did listen to it, and soaked up all of the information contained within it, everything clicked into place. It was everything, i had already knew, and had also read before, but it was put in a way, that just seemed to finalize everything for me, and put into place, the final missing pieces. I purchased the audio version of the book, for my iPhone, i must have listened to the book, nine times in two days. The iPhone made it so easy to listen to these amazing audio books. I started to listen to it, every spare minute i got to myself, in the end i knew it word for word. What he said in the book made me realize what i was doing wrong in my life, i was asking which is fine and ok, but you must have something to give back to the world, you cannot just take in this life. I believe this book, that i am writing now, as i sit at my computer screen, will be my gift to world, i feel that i have been getting nudges, and messages for sometime now, to write about this special life's journey, which his changing my life in so many ways. But i feel, till this point now, i have been mostly ignoring them, and putting these urges to the back of my mind, again missing the important message's, that life is giving to me. I hope this book will find its way, to many different people, from all over our amazing planet, so they too can embark on their own life's journey, and create the life of their true dreams. I truly hope that you, the reader of this book will begin to see human life, for the amazing thing it really is. I also feel that there are millions of people around this planet, asking the same questions which i am trying to answer here. I feel we are all looking for the same missing things, and answers to our life's purpose. I honestly don't know, if winning large amounts of money, would really make me happy, or having huge houses, fast cars, etc. I think, we have all been programmed from a very early age, to just want the material things in this life, i also believe that our judgments are truly clouded by this illusionary, material world. We are all missing the bigger picture, of our lives. There are many people around the world with vast fortunes, but they are still very unhappy with their lives. Don't misunderstand me, i believe you can do great good with money, you can change many things for the better, but there must still be a healthy balance. A lot of people may feel guilty, asking for vast amounts of money houses, cars etc, but another part of the book, by Wallace D Wattles, also stood out to me, it was the fact of not feeling guilty, for asking for the things you really wanted in your life, large or small, this one statement put it all behind me, which comes from the bible, IT WAS YOUR FATHERS PLEASURE TO GIVE YOU THE KINGDOM, SAID JESUS. I believe God wants us all to live the most abundant lives we can dream of, also living the happiest lives, we can too. Its now thought that jesus himself, was also a very wealthy. I believe this is our god given right, and i intended to use it, to improve every area of my life. Days later i was on youtube, and i came across a video, which displayed a man winning the lottery, buying large house's, luxury car's, etc. I later found out through some research, these videos were made, with software form a company called mind movies. What struck me at the time, was the videos contents, it seemed as though the movie was portraying my exact thoughts, back to me. I immediately joined their website, where i could begin to make my own personal mind movies to watch, on my iPhone, iPad, computer's, etc. These personal mind movies were then watched on a daily basis, to enforce your desires onto your subconscious mind. This is how it worked, it was extremely simple, the site was extremely user friendly, and also very professionally designed. The only work on my part, was to add my own personal pictures, for my mind movies. After you added your picture's for the things you wanted, or desired in your life, you could then, also add some powerful affirmations, to further enhance the power of the mind movie video, or if you wanted to, you could use the many template affirmations provided by the mind movies website. Once the mind movie was ready, and you had finished adding all of your pictures, and affirmations, you could then add a personal song of your choice to the mind movie, to really get your emotions, and senses firing, associating all of the good, and positive feelings, with your newly created mind movie. Then when everything was finally added, you had a chance to preview your personal mind movie, checking to see if you really liked the final outcome, and design, before you clicked the final processing button on the web site. Once your mind movie was processed by the site, you could then download the finished mind movie, to all your video playing devices. This was an amazing, and truly genius idea, it give you the opportunity to watch your own personal mind movies, just about anywhere, you wanted to. I have got to say, this is such a simple, but totally brilliant idea, thank you to all of the people at mind movies, for helping many thousands of people, from all around the world, to realize their deepest dreams and desires, in such a simple, and amazing way. Mind movies, have made it possible for anybody, to make the movie of their dreams, giving everybody the chance to start living, and realizing their true dreams. I would personally recommend, that anybody trying to live their dreams, immediately log on to mindmovies.

com, purchase the very reasonable priced software, and start making your own mind movies, and start living your dreams now. The effect on me was dramatic, after one week of watching my personal mind movies, i was starting to have my very vivd dreams again, with myself winning euro millions jackpot, but this time, i was actually seeing myself inside my actual Audi R8 car, parked up outside my dream house, that i had envisioned living in, when i had won the euro millions jackpot. I also started to get strange things happening, i would start to see, and feel my self in the Audi R8, when driving normal cars on road test's at work, i mean, i would start to get flashes of the inside of the Audi R8 car, while driving a normal car on road test. The same thing also started to happen at my house, i would also start to get the same little flashes, and actual glimpses of being in the actually house, the one i had picked on the internet, many months before. I would walk in a room and get a flash of the room, in the house i wanted to buy. At first this was only brief flashes, but as the weeks went by, my dreams got more and more real, and the images, or flashes were lasting longer, and they also seemed to be getting much easier, to keep them in my minds eye. It felt as though, i was starting to move between two totally different set's of realities. This went on for three to four weeks, and i could feel the things i wanted moving towards me, at a much faster pace than ever before. But again it seemed to be right there, within my reach, but it was as though, i was not letting it come in to my life, in someway. This went on for a few more months, and then i hit a brick wall again, i started asking the universe for the answer to what i was missing, it must of been some two or three weeks later, when i was on a new, and exciting business trip to Dubai, with my family members. On this amazing trip, my question, from many weeks earlier was answered, in a dramatic way. After having a wonderful family break, and also a very successful business trip in Dubai, me, my dad, and brother were all in a fantastic moods. We all made our way from the hotel, to Dubai's main airport, where in a few hours we would be setting off for home. While in Dubai airport we were all having a shop for some family present to take home to our wives, and children. As i browsed the many luxury shops, looking for some ideas, of what to buy my waiting family, i strolled past a small book store situated in the end section of the airport shop's. I looked at the book shop, and got a instant churning in my stomach, a gut feeling that i should go inside, and have a look around. I thought to myself, i have not bought a new book for a few weeks, maybe i should get one for the plane ride home. But for some reason, i didn't enter the shop at that time, and i carried on walking straight past. But again with a unusual set of circumstances, my dad seemed to end up in the same book store, i could see him from where i was standing, in the souvenir shop, just opposite the book store. I could hear him shouting across to me, come here i want to show you something. Has i walked into the small book store, i was immediately greeted by my father, asking me to work out the exchange rate, on a book he was thinking of buying. I then said i didn't know how to work out the currency difference, then at that very moment, the assistant from the counter, immediately, and efficiently told him the answer he was looking for. That very second, my attention was immediately drawn to a book shelf, just in front of me. A book some three shelves up from the bottom, seemed again to stand out to me, from all of the other books on the row's of many shelves. It again, seemed to take on, a set of glowing characteristic's. As my eyes, began to focus in on the book, i immediately noticed the secret logo, the logo seemed to stand out to me like a beacon flashing, i run across the shop, to grab it off the shelf. When i held it in my hands, i instantly knew this book had the answer to my question's, that i had been asking, over the last few month's of my life's journey. As i paid for the book, i think even the cashier, picked up on my excitement, of purchasing Rhonda Bryne new, and latest book. I then walked out of the book store with the biggest smile on my face. Me, my dad, and brother then made our way to the airport coffee shop, yep it was my favorite, star bucks, off course. We all sat down together, resting our tired feet, and also indulging in some very refreshing drinks, before our long flight home. My dad, and brother could also see, my new discovered excitement, that the book had brought to me, i feel it was written all over my face. I know my dad, and brother, both thought it was just another book, that had brought this excitement to my face, but for me, it was much more than just the book, that had given me, this new sense of great excitement. To me, it was the mysterious set of circumstances, and the magical happenings, in the past few weeks, that had really excited me. I had a feeling inside of me, that this book held the answer's to some of my recent questions, on my life's journey so far. I felt it was, a truly unmistakable message from god. As i was sat down in Starbucks with my drink, i felt i couldn't wait any longer, it was still an hour or so, till we all got on the plane, to fly home to the UK. At the expense of seeming to be ignorant to my brother, and father, i immediately started to read the first few pages, from the new book by Rhonda Bryne. Just within the first few pages of this new book, i immediately knew, what i had been missing out, of my daily life. I feel the previous book that i had only just read, by Wallace D wattles, the science of getting rich, also tried to tell me, what i had been missing out of my daily life routine, but i totally let it pass me by, at that time. I now believe the part which has been missing in my daily life routine, was the all powerful emotion of GRATITUDE. After reading the first few pages of this amazing new book by Rhonda bryne, called The Magic, i knew deep down within my heart, that i had not really been practicing gratitude at all. I felt i probably had done, for a short time at the very start of my life's journey, but after reading the magic, by Rhonda bryne, i now know that there is so much more to gratitude than just saying thank you, the odd time here, and there. You really have got to be truly grateful, with all of your heart for the things you already have in your life, even if you only have a little in your life, you must still be grateful for that. Once you are truly grateful with all your heart, for what you already have in your life now, only then, can you be showered with more happiness, and greater material abundance in your life. l know this is where i was failing in my life, i was taking too many of the so called material things in my life for granted. I truly thought i was grateful for everything in my life, but when i really started to take a look at myself self, deep down, i really started to see how many things, i was really taking for granted in my daily life, without any thought at all, for how i actual received all of them. Not stopping for a moment, just to consider how lucky, and truly blessed, i already was in my life. At this point, i began to change this immediately, even in the airport at Dubai, i must have said thank you, sixty or so times, before i even entered the plane, for our flight home to the UK. The effect of this constant heart felt Gratitude, for everything in my life, was already starting to have, a truly dramatic effect on myself, and also the many people that i was encountering. I continued to read, the rest of the book on my flight home to the UK, the book seemed like a bit of a refresher course for me, at first. The first part of the book started to point out, and refresh my memory, to a lot of the things, that i had already been practicing in my daily life, and which somewhere along my life's journey, i had forgotten about. I now believe, this is why i hit a sort of brick wall, in my life's journey, but when i started to implement them all over again in my life, with a new sense of energy, and excitement, which this new book started to give me, in abundance, things really started to turn around for me. I also started to implement, some of the new teachings in the book, and the effect was again, total life transforming for me. I studied, and also finished the remaining part of the book, by the end of the plane flight home. When i got home, my family immediately noticed the difference in me, i had a sort of glowing energy, and excitement around my entire being. I felt so excited, and blessed with my new found knowledge, and re-understanding of how life really works. I felt that i had again learnt a very valuable lesson, in the last few weeks of my life's journey. Even though i had not received my material desires, i felt that i had instead, received something much more valuable, than anything a material desire, could ever give me in my life. But i feel at this time, i cannot find the words, to justify, and describe these many new feelings, that i seem to be experiencing at this point in my life's journey. All i know for sure, at this time, is gratitude seems to be the key to true happiness, and abundance in this life, thank you Rhonda Byrne for the many gifts, you have given our world. The weeks seem to go by, and life was getting better, and better by the day, i was using gratitude everywhere in my life, and i have got to be honest here, the urgency of getting my material desires, seemed to have totally left me. I now seemed to be totally content, with what i already had in my life, and also happy with where my life was taking me. I am not saying, i didn't want my desires anymore, but i just seemed to be radiating happiness from the inside, and my desires just didn't seem that important to me anymore. These new feelings of happiness inside of me, i feel i have not felt, since i had been a young child. I don't mean, i have not been happy in my life up till now, but this is a different kind of happiness, the one you get when you are a child, coupled with the discovery, and excitement of life. It is hard to put in to words, but i am sure we have all felt it, at sometime in our lives. Weeks went by, and i thought this must have been what i had been looking for all this time. Maybe, this was my lottery win, it truly did feel as though i had won the jackpot of life. Then late on a friday night, i was sat watching some television, just relaxing after a hards days work, i just seemed to be flicking through the many sky channels that are available these days. I seemed to suddenly stop flicking through the sky channels, and i found my self confronted, with a talk show program. Will Smith was being interviewed, i have always like Will Smith, he seems like a great person, so i decided to watch the interview. Unbelievable the second i began to listen to interview, i heard the words, the law of attraction. I was not sure how the subject, of the law of attraction came up, because i had only just tuned in, and it was already half way through the interview. The interviewer then mentioned a book to Will Smith, called the THE ALCHEMIST, by Paulo Coelho, this book seemed to be one of Will's favorites. When the book was mentioned in the interview, i again seemed to get that feeling, of everything slowing down, and the words seemed to stand out to me. I then knew that i had to read this book by Paulo Coelho. I had come to know this feeling well by now, i was again getting inner guidance, on what direction to take. My first thought was to download the book, from the internet, but for some reason,i just never did it. Two days went by, and i seemed to forget all about the book, by Paulo Coelho. It was a bank holiday weekend, so me, and my family went shopping to our local town centre. After buying a few things, my wife Wendy said, i would like to buy a book, to read in bed at night. I said ok, great lets have a walk around water stones, to see if you like anything. On entering the book store, me and my family were all greeted by a author promoting the release of his new book. At that very moment, i got funny feeling in the pit of my stomach, the one you get when you go on fair rides, it was like a feeling of overwhelming excitement inside of me. When the author approached me, and my family, with a copy of his new book, held in is hand, i instantly knew then, in that very moment, this is what, i would also love to do with my life. I instantly started to picture myself, in my minds eye, doing the same thing, sitting in a book store, promoting the release of my own new book, eventually leading me to the exploration of the wider world, at large. I even said to my wife, you never know, that might be me sitting there some day soon, my wife gave me a nice warming smile, and walked off looking around the book store, for her new book to read at night, while resting in bed. I felt that i was not interested in buying any new books to read, i felt more compelled to write my own book, and jump start a career in something, i truly loved with all my heart. Seeing the author promoting his book, seemed to have given me a new sense of inner creativity. My wife was still browsing the many book shelves, of the book store, me and Kyle also started to look around the book store too. At that point even my son Kyle, wanted a book to read, so we both started to look for one he may like. When my eyes began to scan the very first books shelves, i think you may guess the book, that was staring straight at me, it was THE ALCHEMIST by Paulo Coelho. This was amazing, even though i had not forgotten about this book, i had for some unknown reason, put it to the back of mind, and forgotten about buying it. You guest it, i immediately bought the book, with a feeling of great excitement inside myself, i had again witnessed, the power of this strange unseen force, that guides all our daily lives, in a truly magical way. After also picking a new book for my son, we all made our way to the exit of the book store. Just before i left the book store, i gave my best wishes, to the author, and hoped his new book would be a roaring success, that he thoroughly deserved. I knew then, that it wasn't easy to become an author, and write a successful book, so i had the upmost respect for this man sitting there promoting his own book. I immediately started to read my new book, by Paulo Coelho, i felt i couldn't wait until i even got home. There are probably many of you reading my book now, who have already read the book THE ALCHEMIST, it has already sold a staggering sixty five million copies worldwide, wow!!!. The thing about this fascinating story, that seemed to stand out to me straight away, was the Shepard boy, his story in the book, seemed in a way, to be reflecting exactly what i wanted in my life. He also wanted to travel, and find his treasure in life, he also traveled to Egypt, in search of his treasure. Here again was a similarity to my life's Journey. Egypt was again appearing in my life, i felt that my destiny, past, future and present, was somehow inter-connected, with the greatness of Egypt. It was now getting impossible for me to ignore this anymore, i just had to find some way, to get my self back to the magical, and mysterious land of Egypt. I say back, because i now feel, at sometime in my many life incarnations on planet earth, i have lived in, and also loved Egypt with all of my heart, and something is now drawing me back there, just like it had drawn the shepherd boy in the book, THE ALCHEMIST. Weeks later my wife returned home from work, saying she wanted to book a summer holiday, and where would i like to go. I explained i would love to go to Egypt, she could see in my eyes i was very passionate about it, but she said that Cairo, and the pyramids was not the place, to take the children on holiday. I totally understood her reservations, and i knew myself, that it wasn't the place for a family holiday. I never pushed the matter with her, and suggested to her, that she should get some new travel brochures, from our local travel agents, so we could have a good look through them before we made up our minds. That week, Wendy picked up some of the latest holiday brochures from the travel agents, the weekend eventually came, so we decided to have a look through them together. We immediately came across Sharm El Sheikh, a part of Egypt, which has been built, just for the tourist industry. We were both blown away, by what we were seeing, it looked amazing, it was also great for the kids, there were great family attractions, like water parks, family beaches, it looked more than perfect. Wendy then found out, that one of her auntie's, had been to Sharm El Sheikh many times before, for their own holidays. When Wendy contacted her auntie to find out, if it was suitable for a family holiday, to my surprise the resort we were thinking of booking, was the one Wendy's auntie, had stayed in many times before. They both got talking about Egypt on the phone, and Wendy's auntie explained she loved the place, and she had also visited the Great Pyramids of Gizza. I said how was that possible, it is hundreds of miles away from the Great Pyramids of Gizza, she then explained you can fly there from Sharm El Sheikh, it only takes one hour, and you can be back in the resort of Sharm El Sheikh, by the night time. I then knew this was again, the work of this mysterious unseen force, to get me to where i felt, i needed to go. Two days later, it was all booked including a day trip for me, and my mother in law to the Great Pyramids Of Gizza, she had also been fascinated by the Great Pyramids of Egypt. What i now knew to be true from all of this, is that my life's journey is a constantly unfolding magical mystery, created in part, by our own vast consciousness. I felt that at last, i was finally getting some of the answers to the many questions, i had been asking, along my life's journey. I am not sure what treasure's if any, Egypt holds for me, but i feel my entire soul, being drawn to this ancient, and mysterious place. Deep within myself, i know that it will be another great life changing event for me, good or bad, i don't yet know. But i know, i must follow my destiny, soon i feel i will be returning home in some way, as strange, has that may sound. In the next few months of my life, i will be preparing myself for what ever is awaiting for me, at the Great Pyramids of Egypt. In last few days, i have come across a new, and amazing book. I feel that i have discovered this new book, just at the right time, in my life's journey. It again, seemed to bring all of the books, that i had already read, over the past few years, into a new sense of meaning, and understanding. This book would have never made sense to me, if i had read it at the beginning of my life's journey. I again believe i was guided to this book, at the prefect time, to make perfect sense of everything up till this point. in my life's journey so far. It as shed new light on everything for me, it is a must read for everybody, but i feel it can only be read, when you are ready to read it on your own life's journey, the book is called Your Faith is Your Fortune, By Neville Goddard. Please only read this when you feel you have been guided to it, you will know yourself, when the time is right for you. With these many new insights in my life, i now feel i have a new understanding, of how life really works. I feel that i have been trying to force things to happen in my life, being to fixated, by my many material wants, that seem to fill our earthly lives. I now feel, and know, that we truly can have anything we want in our life, but there is one condition to this. Our desire's in this material life, cannot be in conflict, with our true life's purpose, this time around, on planet earth. I believe this is why many people, from around our planet, discard the notion of the law of attraction, as a total fantasy. Many people including myself, desire many material things in life, that totally conflicts, with their true life's purpose this time around. These internal conflict's between your material, and spiritual needs, will only lead to sadness, illness, and even death, in extreme cases. I have now come to a point in my life, where i can feel the conflict inside of me, between my spiritual needs, and my material desires. If i had won the lottery, i now know i wouldn't probably be writing this book now, or i wouldn't have discovered many of life's gift's, and hidden secrets. It would have sent me down, the totally wrong path for me, this time around, just accepting these simple fact's is truly refreshing to say the least. All i am try to say, is take a look, at your deepest dreams, and desires, and make sure they are not in conflict with your true life purpose this time around. This will save you lots of pain, and wasted time in your life, giving you the chance to discover your true life's purpose, much earlier on, in your life time here on this planet. In the next few chapters of this book, i have included detailed interpretations of the vivid dreams i have had, while sleeping, and also in deep meditation. The first dream is about winning the lottery down to the finest details, the second is a very vivid dream about Egypt. I am not quite sure why i have included them both here is this book, but i feel that they have both, played an important part in my life's journey, so i feel that i must include both of them, so that the full story is told, in every detail. At this point i must stress again, these are only my dreams, at this point in time.

CHAPTER 24

Recurring Dreams 1,
The Lottery Win

My dream always starts with me, checking my emails on my iPhone, while sitting at home watching tv. As i look through my in box of messages, i notice a email from my online lottery account, informing me, they had some news about a ticket i had bought online, some days earlier. Having had many of these message's, from the lottery over the years, i knew the script very well. It would tell me to log into my online lottery account, saying it had news about a ticket, i had bought for what ever draw date, it was referring to. But this time, it was different, i had a funny feeling in my stomach, the email time at the top of the page seemed to stand out, it had arrived at my email account, at approximately 3.35am, which had never happened before. It usually arrives much later in the day, when the much smaller prizes, had all been processed. So with great excitement, i immediately logged into my online lottery account. There i was immediately confronted with my account balance, in top right hand corner of the computer screen. To my astonishment there it was, the exact amount of money, i had been asking for, £96,000,497,048. My heart was beating like a drum, my mouth went dry, the room fell into a complete silence, and then everything seemed to stop. Everything slowed to a complete halt, i thought time itself had stopped. I could even hear my own heart beating, i knew then, at that very moment, this was going to change me, and my families lives forever. I also knew that this win, happening under these circumstances, was going to change so many other peoples lives, from all around the planet. I was going to share this secret knowledge, that i had used to manifest, all of my deepest dreams, and desires. I was going to tell the world about the special secret regarding the law of attraction, proving to wider world, that you really can have anything you want in this life. But i also knew that i had won this money for a special purpose, i felt that i must spread the word to everyone around the planet, hoping that i could empower them, with this information too, just the way it had done for me. I knew from that point on, i was going to do great things with this vast amount of money. I also knew this vast amount of money, came with great responsibility. This money would help me to spread this valuable information, and knowledge that i had been collecting over the past few years, and months of my life's journey. I immediately composed my self, and also my thoughts, i then awoken my family, and told them about this life changing news. They were also in a state of utter shock, and also disbelief for some time. The most amazing part for me, was what my son Kyle said to me, straight away, he said i always believed you would do it dad, Kyle truly never stopped believing in me, thank you son. My wife Wendy, and my daughter Danielle were so taken back, not just by the lottery win, but the win being the same amount, i had said, i was going to win for such a long time. After we all had time to reflect, and calm ourselves down, we discussed as a family, what we would do next. I explained that i had to share this valuable lottery win, and also the information, and knowledge, that i had collected over the last two years of my life. I said that i wanted to share this win with as many people as i possibly could.

I knew going public with the win, would help me to do all of this, and it would also give me the chance to spread the news all around the planet. We immediately contacted camelot to verify our win, and arranged for the collection of our winnings. I told them immediately, that i wanted to go public, straight away, they seemed pleased with that news, because its good publicity for them too. My wife Wendy, was still a bit worried that going public, with such a large amount of money, she thought that it may put us all in harms way, but i reassured her, that it was the right thing to do. I knew it was right, i felt it from deep inside of myself, and i also felt this was always our path to follow. This was the first time i saw it, in Wendy's eyes, she knew at that point, that what i had been saying all along, was all true, and she never doubted me from that point on. The press conference, was set for the coming tuesday, and i prepared myself with a speech. I also brought my copy of the book the secret, to the press conference. We arrived at the press conference venue, a few hours before the main media were due to arrive, this would give us plenty of time, to prepare ourselves, for the coming press conference ahead. I also wanted to discuss with Camelot, what i was going to say to the waiting press conference. I explained to the camelot representative, in a brief, but detailed story, about the amazing set of events, leading up to this amazing jackpot win. I included as many details as i could, within the short period of time, that i had. Explaining the magical set of circumstances surrounding this lottery win, including the role of the book the secret. I also explained, that i had been on a truly amazing, and life changing journey, leading up to this very point. I basically gave her the heads up, on what i as going to say to the waiting press conference. I have got to be honest, she seemed quite taken back by it all. I don't think she knew what to say, or even what to make of it all. There was a deadly silence in the room for about five minutes, and i wasn't sure what to say, but it was my press conference, and i was determined, to tell them my story, the way it actually happened to me, and my family. It was about ten minutes to go, and my nerves were really starting to kick in, they are all going to think i have lost the plot, or gone mad, but the voice inside of me was saying, you know what you have to do, and i knew i had to do it. Another five minutes went by, then Wendy and i, followed by the Camelot representative, both walked out to the waiting media. We all sat down at the waiting press table, i had the secret book in my hand, it all started with a barrage of question form the waiting media. There were lots of camera flashes, coming from every direction, after a couple of minutes the camera flashes seemed to stop, which i was very glad about. I slowly regained my sight back, from the blinding camera flashes, i then started to answer the media questions one by one. One of the media's questions, led me to my perfect opportunity, to tell them how i had come to win this mega jackpot amount. I started by telling them i had been on a two year life changing journey, and the book i held here in my hands was the start of it all. They seemed a bit taken back, by what i was saying, then all at once they started firing questions at me. What journey, whats that book your holding, who wrote it, i then told them a short, but detailed story, about the last two years of my life. They were all listening quietly at first, but when i had finished telling them my short story, with my brief explanations, they all charged me again with a barrage, of questions. I then explained it was not possible to answer all of their questions here, but i did urge anybody who was interested, to read this life changing book, that i held within my hands, and start to apply these special secret's, into their own lives. I had also brought along a surprise for the waiting media, it was nine copies of the secret, to pass out, around to anybody who wanted a copy. They were all immediately snapped up. I then explained i had been writing my own book, to document this amazing life's journey, that i had been on, which i would be releasing soon, when i could find a publisher willing to publish it. On Returning home from the lottery media conference, to our surprise, we found that the media, had already found out where we lived. The next day we found that the story was being covered, in all the lager news papers. This was great, this was exactly what i wanted. I wanted as many people to find out about this truly valuable, and life changing information, and start use it for themselves. Days went by, and i was getting messages left on my iPhone, from different people, saying they would be interested in publishing my book, could i contact them to arrange a meeting, to discuss it with them. But i already had plans, who i wanted to publish my book with. It was Hay House Publishing, who had published a great deal of the books, which i had read over the course of my two year, life changing journey. I got some contact details off their website, and i had a conversation with a member of the Hay House staff. To my great surprise, they had already heard about my story from the press, and was interested in looking at my book. They ask me if i could send them a couple of chapters by email, and they booked me an appointment in London, for one week later. This was a very exciting time for me, this is what i have always wanted, deep down, just to help people, and i think this book, was a great start in that direction. I then set about contacting two charities, which i promised myself i would do, when i won this large amount of money, and i knew i could make a meaningful difference to their lives. I watched a Tv documentary two years ago, with Ross Kemp presenting, he visited Palestine, and there was a charity there looking after orphaned children from the Israeli, and Palestinian conflict. These children had lost both of their parents to this conflict. They were left deeply traumatized, and their bravery left a lasting impression on me. I said once i had the means to do something meaningful for them, i would do all i could to help these children. The other charity was again from the same Tv documentary with Ross Kemp, it was filmed in Nigeria, where very young children, were left to care for themselves on garbage tips. They were left totally alone, sniffing glue all day long, and dying at a very early age, from doing this. These two events in my life, touched my heart deeply, i could not believe that this was happening, in the twentieth century. I contacted itv immediately to see if i could meet with them, to find a way to get the much needed money, and resources, to these brave, and amazing young children. Hoping that i could change their lives for the better. The lottery was also very helpful, in helping me to contact, all of the relevant people, and two days later a meeting was set up with itv, where we discussed plans to visit these locations, and find a way to help these many suffering children. But i still new, my main purpose was to spread this message around the world to every body i could, and i knew winning this vast amount of money, in these amazing set of circumstances, would help me greatly. Days later i set up meetings with the press, who were very eager for my full story, which i would greatly give them, in the form of my new book. I feel this is now only the start of my life's journey, even though i have lived on this earth for nearly fourty years, i feel i have only just found my life's path, and true purpose, and i am excited for the future of the human race. We are living in amazing times, and i believe we have all been in a form of conscious sleep for a long time, but it seems, that now we are all starting to awake, from this deep sleep, and the future for humanity, is looking much more brighter than ever before.

CHAPTER 25

Recurring Dream 2, Egypt

In the past two years of my life's journey, Egypt has started to fill many of my night time dreams. These dreams started to intensify themselves, the closer it got to my planned, family holiday to Egypt. In these very vivid, and real like dreams, i could actually see myself, stood at the footings stones of the Great Pyramids of Gizza. The excitement was starting to fill my entire body, with feelings of new life force energy, entering into my body. I felt as though i was nineteen years old again. My family was also excited by the pending holiday to Egypt, but i feel for them, it was just another holiday in the sun. It must of been only a week to go before the actual holiday, i was sitting at home reading a book, just relaxing lying back on the sofa, with my feet up. My family members, were all out, doing their own different things, i felt a little tired, and i could feel myself, drifting into a relaxing state of meditation. The meditation started just like all of the other meditations, that i had been doing over the last few months of my life. I had noticed, a few more interesting aspects to my meditations lately, but i did not think anything more about it, and i just put it down to my expanding awareness, about life. I had been seeing more burst of light, and lot more of the whitish swirling mist, which i had mentioned in the earlier chapters of this book. But this meditation session, turned out to be totally different. After about ten minutes into the meditation, i knew something was different, i could feel a sort of pushing upwards of my body, and every hair on my body began to stand on its end. I also began to see deep blue pulsating shape's, changing themselves in to blob like structures, these were all still visible, even when my eyes's were open. At first these new visions's, and sensations, were quite frightening to say the least, i even opened my eyes a few times, and closed them again, to see if they went away. But these new visions, and sensations did not go away, eventually everything in the room seemed to be glowing, and the shapes of the different objects in the room, seemed to look tall and thin, it's quite hard to explain, i seemed to be in a sort of euphoric state of mind. It was amazing, from being scared at first, and then not wanting to come out of this state of mind at all. It was quite a roller coaster of emotions to go through, in a such a short period of time. These sensations went on for about another five minutes, then the phone rang in the hall way, sending a strong echo of the ring through the hall way, and into the room where i lay. This ringing noise, then seemed to bring me back from the deep meditation state of mind, that i was in. In the last few meditation sessions, i have tried again to get these new sensations back again, but i have not been able to do so. We are set to fly to Egypt in the next few days, and i feel, somehow this is all connected to my coming trip, to the mysterious land of Egypt. The days seemed to pass very quickly, the morning of the holiday was upon us, we were all ready for the off, all truly looking forward to our holiday ahead, which i knew, would fill all of our lives with new adventure, and wonder. We arrived at the holiday resort in Egypt on the Monday morning, the weather was beautiful, in fact the whole place, had a magical feel about it. When we checked in the hotel, i also excitedly confirmed my trip details, for my flight to Cairo, to see the Great Pyramids of Gizza. All the details were fine, confirming to me that i would be flying out on the coming thursday, for my trip to the Great Pyramids of Gizza. By this time my mother in law had changed her mind, saying that she did not want to go on the trip to the Pyramids, she felt that she did not want to leave the children, on their holiday. Somewhere inside of me, i already knew, that this trip was for me alone, so i gladly accepted her decision, for the best for everybody. The few days that i had with my family, before my trip to the Great Pyramids of Gizza, were truly fantastic, i got to spend some precious time, with my amazing family, and the weather was glorious. My children were in their element, and they just loved all of the many swimming pools, and water slides, that our holiday resort had on offer, everything was just perfect. I was set to fly to Cairo the next morning about 4.00am, the flight would take about one hour. When i arrived in Cairo, i would be met by a representative of the company, who i had booked the excursion with. He would be dropping me off at the Great Pyramids of Gizza, and later in the evening, he would also be picking me back up for the later flight home that evening, back to the resort of Sharm El Sheikh. In the short taxi ride to the Pyramids of Gizza, from the airport, something started to happen to me, at first i started to get a spinning sensation, and everything seemed to spin inside the taxi. I also started to get a feeling of being light, almost like my body was beginning to float. At first, i just thought it may have been the effects of the heat, combined with the short plane flight across the desert. But as i sat there in the back of the taxi, i realized, it was not that hot at all, it was still very early on in the morning. The feelings started to subside themselves, and my tour guide who was sitting in the passenger side of the vehicle, told me that we should be at the Pyramids, in about thirty minutes or so. I then just laid my self back on to the seat of the taxi, and tried to relax myself, for a short while. The driver of the vehicle didn't seem to have much to say, and he spoke only broken bits of english. At that point, the vehicle came to a abrupt stop, i looked out of the side window, there seemed to be some sort of accident, on the road just in front of us, which started to cause a small traffic jam. We stayed parked up in traffic jam, for about ten minutes. I manage to ask my guide, how far away the Great Pyramids of Gizza was, he said, what i understood to be about fifteen minutes away. Then without warning, i started to get a mild itching, and also a heating up of both of my forearms, it seemed to be right on the part of my forearms, where many years before, i had two tattoos done of Egyptian hieroglyphics. This was really strange, every other part of my forearms, was fine, it wasn't painful, it was just noticeable. The hieroglyphics, started to go slightly red in colour, i didn't know what to make of it, at all. I started to hear, the beeping of car horns, in front of us, then as i looked up, i could see, the Great Pyramids of Gizza. This immediately pulled my attention away from my forearms. I find it hard at this point, to explain in words, what i felt, when i first seen the Great Pyramids of Gizza. Even though i could only see the Pyramids in the distance, it still took me by great surprise, almost taking my breath away. My heart started beating faster in excitement, i started to get a tingling sensation all over my body. When the taxi i was in, eventually pulled up to the drop point, for the gathering groups of tourists, i immediately left the vehicle, and arranged to meet him, and the driver back at the same point, about five o'clock that evening. I started to walk towards the Great Pyramids, with a few other tourists, who had arrived on buses, at the same time, has me. It seemed to be a five minute walk to the actual base of the Great Pyramids themselves, i started talking to an American couple, who had just arrived in Cairo like myself. They also had a aura of excitement, and wonder about them. I think it must of taken us about ten minuets, to get to the base of the Great Pyramids, half way through the walk, John my new American friend, commented about my hieroglyphics tattoos, that i had on both of my forearms. He also commented on them, being a glowing red colour, i explained it wasn't sunburn, and i wasn't sure why they had gone so red. The closer i got to the Great Pyramids, i started again with the spinning feeling, and also with a sense of euphoria. But this time, these strange feelings were also accompanied with what i would call flashing pictures, of different realties. I was seeing visions of the Great Pyramids, in their glory days, i mean the actual time they were built thousands of years before. I could even see the ancient people, walking about, covered in all types of exotic outfits.

Then in a split second, my reality would seem to flash back to the present day reality. It was all getting to much, my head was spinning from these visions, i needed to sit myself down, for a few minutes, and close my eyes, trying to recompose myself, and gather my thoughts, and try to work out, what was really happening to me. On the re-opening of my eyes, after a few minutes, the images seemed to stop, but i still had the spinning feeling slightly, but i felt ok in myself. I stood to my feet, and looked around me, there weren't many people about, it was still very early in the morning. My new american friend, John was nowhere to be seen. I decided to gather my senses, and set off walking towards the tourist entrance in the Great Pyramid. Once i showed my pass, i was able to get into the make shift entrance of the Pyramid. Once i was inside this amazing structure, the images returned with an even greater intensity. I became frightened, i now couldn't seem to return myself, to the present day reality, these new visions seemed to be my present reality now, and i couldn't seem to come out of them. I then saw two figures approaching me, from a distant passage way, of some kind. They were dressed in, what i would call short robes, of some kind, decorated with bright coloured symbols, this was very easy to see, the whole area was very brightly lit. But i am not sure by what, i could not see any light source, of any kind. The symbols on the robes were very beautiful in their design, but i still couldn't make them out, at this time, or if they had any meaning to them. When the approaching figures, got within five feet from me, they stopped, and spoke to me in a language, i thought i had never heard before now, but for some strange reason, i totally understood every word they said to me. They were asking me to follow them, i don't know why, but i felt a sense of trust with these two strangers, even though i did not recognize their faces, i still felt i knew them, in some way. I followed them closely down a narrow sort of hallway, all the walls were beautiful decorated, with coloured hieroglyphics. We passed many different people in the hallway, nobody spoken a word to me, even though they were looking straight at me, has i passed them by, in this narrow hall way. We eventually came to a junction section, one pathway led upward, on a incline, the other pathway, which we all followed, went downward into an underground opening. I could see that this vast corridor, went on, for as far as my eyes could see, it was again brightly lit, by a unseen light source. We eventually stopped, at a wonderful water feature, there were figures of gold in the centre of the water feature, they shone very brightly, it was almost blinding to look at them. I was able to sit, and rest my feet by the side of this great water feature, my two guides, also sat down next to me. The water also seemed to carry a beautiful calming smell to it. My two guides, both talked between each other, i only picked up on a few words, that they were saying to each other. I eventually picked up from there conversation, that they were both some sort of priest's, of some kind, and i also kept hearing the same name, Amun, they seemed to be using the name, over and over again, in there conversation. I thought i must be dreaming or asleep, but it was real, i touched the walls of the corridors, and they was cold to my touch. At that point, my guide's again, ask me to follow them, which i gladly did. We got about two hundred yards into the corridor, and out of a door way, we were joined by two tall guards, i called them guards, because they were both carrying weapons, spear like weapons, made of gold like material, or maybe it was gold. They spoke to my priest guides, and then they followed behind me, as we all continued to walk down the hallway. At this point, i should have been absolutely petrified, but i wasn't, i seemed totally calm, and content with where i was, and i don't no why. We must have walked for some fifteen minutes, or so, then we came to door way, leading to a very large open expanse, the room was very well lit, with a bright light, i looked around to see where the light was coming from, but i could not see any signs of illumination devices. The vast room, was filled with many different water features, they were again filled with brightly coloured figures, some of the figures i knew, the other's i had never seen anything like them before. The walls that i could see, were filled with pictures, and drawings, lots of them were of planets, galaxies and the universe. I could see four young women, in Egyptian like dress, sitting on one of the many water feature's. Then from the far corner of the room, five more figures ,appeared from a concealed door way, one of the figures, sat on a sort of chair like structure, the two priest's again ask me to follow them. We were closely followed by the guards behind me. When i eventually got closer to the five figures, on the other side of the room, their faces were starting to come into my view. The man sat on the chair like structure, seemed very important, he was dressed in robes, laced with gold like material. He seemed very tall, even though he was sat down. He was also wearing a silver like band, around the top of his forehead, it had a white glow to it. The men, and women around him always bowed every time they approached him, or even spoken to him. I was brought to only a few feet away from this man, one of the priest's ask me if i knew why i was here, i replied i am not sure why i am here, but i have felt compelled to come to the Great land of Egypt, at this time. The man who was seated on the chair like structure, then replied to me in a firm, but peaceful voice, saying that it had always been your destiny to come here, it was preordained many thousands of years before, that you would arrive here at this time, on this day, of this year. The man on the chair then stood up, and ask me to approach him, he lifted up both of my arms, and looked at the hieroglyphics tattoos on each of my forearms. Has he touched my arms, i felt a surge of energy run through my entire body. I then also noticed, that the redness, and itching had left both of my forearms totally. He said the hieroglyphics on my arms, were a sequence, a key to a hidden chamber, that had been lost by humanity. He said we hadn't much time, and i would not be able to stay here in this reality-dimension, for much longer. He further explained to me, that this hidden chamber held the secrets to the universe, and all life itself. It held the answers to ever question, the human race had ever asked itself. He then said it was my responsibility to re-discover the lost chamber, in my present day reality, because it would save humanity, from what was going to unfold in the next few decades, on our planet. I ask him his name, and why i had been chosen, he said is name was Amun, and he was not from this earth, he had come to this planet many thousands of years ago. He said that he loved humanity, with all of his being, and he had now made this planet his own home. He made it clear to me, that i had chosen this destiny many life times ago, i had agreed to come back here at this time, and place, to complete this destiny. He said this was why, i had felt compelled, and drawn to come here, at this time, and point in space, to complete my destiny, and duty to all of humanity. At that point i started to feel the room spinning again, he said your being pulled back to your own reality, we hadn't much time, follow me quickly. We all ran through a doorway, down another corridor, and came to a entrance point. He said this leads under the Great Sphinx structure, there you will find the chamber, with a large door full of writings, in hieroglyphics. You must be carful in your own reality, it will be dark, and possibly flooded with water, you will need to enter a key sequence, which is on both of your forearms arms. You must do this when you get to the doorway, in the sequence of left to right first. You must be carful not to get it wrong, if you do, it will collapse the whole chamber on top of you. At that point we embraced, and he gave me a small gold scarab, he said this will guide you in your life, when nothing else can. Then i felt a strong spinning feeling, and i was then up to my knees in water, i was in total darkness, i then remembered, i had my iPhone with me, i took it out of my back pack, and put it into torch mode. I could then see that i was in a vast chamber of sorts, i walked around looking for the doorway Amun had mentioned to me, but the room was vast, and the smell of some sort of fumes, was making my eyes water. I continued to walk aimlessly, and then the scarab Amen had given to me, started to make a high pitched noise, i removed it from my pocket, and one of the gems on it seemed to be lighting up. I looked straight ahead, and there was a small light in front of me. I made my way through the knee deep water, but as i started to get closer to the small light in front of me, the water raised to my waist height. Eventually i could see it was the doorway Amun had spoken about. I shone my iPhone torch in front of me, he was right, the door was full of hieroglyphics markings. I looked for the ones, that were the same as the ones on my forearms arms, it took me a while, but i eventually found them all, they were in all different locations, all over the vast door. I started to shake from the cold water around my body, i started to press the hieroglyphics one by one, as i eventually got to the last one, i paused in fear, if i get it wrong, it would be the end of me, and possibly all of humanity. I again held the scarab in my hands, i instantly knew that everything would be ok, i could almost hear Amun's voice in my head, telling me to press the last symbol. I paused thinking, i really hope i had done it in the right sequence. I then pressed the last one, nothing seemed to happen at first, then i could hear a deep rumbling sound, and the water level was starting to drop fast, then the large doors cracked, and moaned, but they eventually started to pull themselves open. After about two minutes the door was fully opened, and the water had totally gone. I also noticed that the strong smell had left the room. I started to walk inside, it was again brightly lit, but i could not see where from, the room was vast in size, and on the side of the walls, there were row's, and row's of large books. There was a sort of fountain, that lay ahead of me, as i approached it, it wasn't water, it was a blue mist, or energy coming out of it, and swirling around a central core of some kind. Then i heard a great noise come from the centre of the core, i looked up, and there it was, straight ahead of me, it was unbelievable. I then knew, this was the answer to everything, everything we had lived, and strived for, in our human existence here on this planet. To be continued!!!!!

CHAPTER 26

Discovering The Healing Power
Contained within us all

A fter all of the strange, and wonderful things, that have filled my life in the last few years, i now feel that my life's journey is beginning to turn full circle. I feel that i am again returning to my destiny, of healing. In the last few months, everything has been going great in my life, but i now feel a new awakening inside of myself. I feel that i am about to embark, on a new direction, towards what i have always known to be my life's purpose, and also my true destiny, here on this planet. When i now look back through my life, healing in different disguises, and forms, has seemed to follow me the whole way through my entire life. Until this point, in my life's journey, i feel that i have been ignoring these many feelings, and thoughts, hiding them away, deep inside of myself. I feel now, that i am ready to move to this next step, in my life's journey, having been shown the way in the last few days, i feel a sense of great excitement, and also achievement. I look forward to the road of new magical discoveries, that lie ahead of me, in my vast, and unwinding life's journey so far. It was a very sobering incident, two days ago, when i finally discovered, the magical healing power's that lies within my body. I now know that this healing power, is a part of all of us, here on this planet, and also the wider universe at large. I truly believe that we all have this magical gift of healing, we just need to re-discover it, within ourselves. Once awakened, it will begin to fill your life, with joy, happiness, abundance, and also health. My son Kyle, had been playing football the weekend just gone, he had pulled a muscle in is right leg, it was nothing to serious, but it was aching, and causing him, a bit of discomfort. It was tuesday evening, i was sitting in my sons room watching television with him, like we did on most evenings, out of the blue he ask me if i could stop is leg from aching. At first i didn't know what to say to him, then a new feeling from inside of me, urged me to place my two hand's on the aching area of his right leg. At first i felt nothing, then about thirty seconds later, my hands, and also my son's leg began to heat up, and turn a slight reddish colour. He immediately said to me, its getting hot dad, i said i know son. I ask him how it felt, he said, i can feel a tingling sensation coming from inside my leg, by this time it was getting quite hot. I know sometimes when you place your hands on someones body, it can heat up, but this was different, it was really, really hot. I left my hands on his leg, for a further five minutes, or so, continuing to watch my son's reactions the whole way through. I then removed my hand's from his leg, and i immediately ask him how it felt, i remember him saying, that it felt much better, he also said he felt sleepy, so i turned off his television, and off he went to sleep. I then walked across the hall way, and sat in my own bedroom, i seemed to sit there for a while, just looking at both of my hands, i also seemed to remember, a tingling like sensation in both of my hands, and they were also slightly reddish to look at. I think at first, i felt quite shocked at what had just taken place, in my son's room. Where had these new sensations come from, was i really a healer of some kind, had i just healed my son, what did all this mean. I immediately started to google the words, healing with hands, vast amounts of information came up onto my iPhone. At this late hour, i just couldn't digest it all, i felt that i also needed to sleep, i got myself ready for bed, and as my head hit the pillow, i was out like a light. When i awoken the next morning, my son was already awake, i thought to myself, i will not mention last night to him, i will just try to gauge, a none judgmental reaction from him, but the first words out of his mouth, truly astounded me, he said thank you, for healing my leg last night dad, my leg really does feel, so much better, thank you. I gave him the biggest hug, and smile, also thanking him for his true innocence's, and honesty. These simple words of honesty, from my son, boosted the confidence, of my entire being, just the thought, that i could help people, with only my healing hands, seemed to fill me, with a sense of gratitude, and bewilderment to my entire core. I felt so very special, and also so privileged that i had been guided, and shown the true healing power, that lied within us all. Now i had the chance to use this power, and begin to build on these new skills, using them, for the better good of all mankind. In the exciting days that followed, i began to research healing, more, and more, it turned out that healing with the hands, was as old as humanity itself. It seemed that somewhere along our ancient history, we had forgotten the true healing power that lied inside all of us. Only in the last decades, or so, have we began to re-discover this hidden power that lies within us all. I was eager, and i wanted to use this healing power again, i could feel it inside of me, swirling around my entire body. I felt that i had a new feeling of energy, filling my body, with the life force of the universe, invigorating my entire being. I began to feel its new power, within the palms of my hands, it was like once i had re-discovered it, it kept nudging me, and growing inside of me, letting me know, it was there, and getting stronger. Kyle my son, was very clever, and also very understanding, he already knew that i had discovered something inside of myself. He also knew that i needed to develop my new found power, he gladly offered himself, has a willing volunteer. I felt very honored, and grateful, for is amazing understanding, i love him dearly with all my heart. I already knew through my many days of research, that no harm could ever come to him, through the use of this magical healing power, in fact, it would only enhance the flow of his own life force energy, giving his body, a boost of this vital life force, that flows through all of our bodies. I needed this to reassure myself, that i could not mistakenly harm anybody, with my newly discovered power. With my further research, i started using my hand's to scan the human body for imbalance's. I did this by placing my hands, palms's down, just above the body, then moving my hands up, and down the body, to see if i could feel, any sensations in either of my hands. I immediately discovered that i could feel a magnetic type of sensation, from all over the body, it was like the feeling of pushing two opposing magnets together. It was a really strange, but a very exciting feeling indeed. I also discovered that my son Kyle, could also feel these strange sensations, when i would move my hands over his body, he said it felt like something was touching his skin, but he could see that my hands were two, or three inches away from his body. I myself, also began to sense, and feel these new, and invisible forces, that seemed to be coming from the palms of my hands. In the days that followed, i began to place my hands, on my own body, on one particular evening, i came home form work with a slight headache, accompanied also with a slight runny nose, which i had been carrying for a few days or so. I was in no way unwell, but i could feel that my body, was fighting off some sort of virus. I thought to myself, why not try to use these newly discovered healing power's, to help relieve my body, from these annoying, and discomforting symptoms. I laid my self back, into a comfortable position on my sofa, i then closed my eye's, and started to relax, just like i had done, on my many meditation sessions. I immediately began to feel, deep pulsations in the palms, of both of my hands, i then knew that all i needed to do, was place both of my hands, on certain points of my body, to help relieve any symptoms that i had, at this time. I started off by placing both hands, on my temple, and crown area, i immediately felt, the same pulsation feeling inside of my head, it wasn't at all painful, or uncomfortable, in fact it felt quite relieving. Then after a few minutes, my slight bodily illness began to start subsiding. At that same time, i seemed to get a slight feeling of light headiness, followed by a very deep sense of inner peace-fullness. My whole body, just seemed to sigh into its self, leaving my body with a feeling of deep inner relaxation. I then moved my palms down to my chest area, i immediately started to get a feeling of water running through my entire chest area, it was an amazing, but strange feeling indeed. It also felt wet, but there was no water to be seen. I did not know what to make of these new feelings, but they felt extremely nice, and also very relaxing. At that point to my total shock, my headache had totally vanished, i couldn't even detect my runny nose either, i was totally blown away by this newly discovered power, that had totally eradicated my bodily illnesses, in minutes wow!!. These new developments give me a new understanding of who i really was, and what i needed to do with my life. After these new healing incidents, i felt very eager to heal, more and more, i felt drawn to it. My next healing incident was my wife Wendy. Lately Wendy had been getting a few headache's, she worked long hours in front of computer screen's, these long hours in front of computer screen's, were making her feel extremely tense, and quite stressed out at times. On this particular evening, Wendy had arrived home late from work, and her head was still pounding from her daily activities. I offered my help, but i knew Wendy was very skeptical, and would immediately resist my offerings, so i left it at that. I feel that you cannot force anybody, into doing anything, that they are not completely comfortable with, i feel that this would only bring on negative situations, in turn cancelling out any positive energy, that i would be trying to create for her. I learnt this very quickly, the person you are trying to heal, must always be willing, and not forced into it, against their own will. I strongly believe that we only channel this life force energy through ourselves, we don't actually create it our selves. Later that evening while, we were lying in our bed, i could still see that Wendy was still in some considerable discomfort, but i never mentioned it to her. Then from nowhere, Wendy ask me to try and get rid of her headache. I felt extremely honored by this, this was definitely not like Wendy, and she must of been in extreme pain, to ask me for help. I asked her to lay back, and try to relax herself, i knew Wendy found relaxing quite difficult to do, this was just the way she was. I placed my hands around her forehead, i instantly felt the heat from my hands, i could also feel the deep throbbing sensations, coming from Wendy's head, and also my hands. I knew Wendy could also feel these sensations, it showed on her facial expressions. After about ten minutes, my hands, and also Wendy's head cooled considerably, the throbbing also disappeared. When Wendy opened her eyes, i instantly knew her headache had gone. I did not ask her to confirm this, i didn't need to, it was written all over her face, i just felt privileged, and grateful, that i could help her in this way. She then went off silently to sleep, then to my surprise, when Wendy awoken the next day, she had a new feeling of energy, and glow about her entire being. I don't think she put this down to the healing, but it didn't matter, i was just happy to see her smiling, and full of energy again. These new experiences, were giving me the confidence to look for new direction in my life, i felt again excited by life, waiting for the next opportunity, to use, and also help the next person who needed it. I knew that i needed to look further into this path of healing, i started to look for new signs, and pointer's along my healing path, it only took a few days, then i knew there was no going back from this point on.

CHAPTER 27

Healing Path Followed Reiki

Has i began to look further into the phenomena, of healing with the hands, i came across an ancient art of healing called Reiki. Some ten years earlier in my life, this same healing modality, seemed to appear out of nowhere, but at this time of my life, i just brushed it off, like it was a silly nonsense, thinking that there was nothing to it. But this time i knew different, i felt like Reiki had re-discovered me somehow, i also felt that i was now ready to re-discover it, at this point in my life. I did some more research into Reiki, at first through the wealth of information circulating the internet, i then later purchased a book to fill in a few blanks, and to clarify some outstanding details for myself. I felt that i needed to research, and also discover what this ancient art was all about, and how it had its place in the healing of the human body, and also the mind. The more i read, and discovered about this ancient art, i couldn't help but think, that in some way, i was already using it. I felt that somewhere inside me, i was already channeling this healing power, in some form, or other. The more facts i discovered, the more i wanted to get involved in Reiki. The first thing i needed to do was get myself attuned, by a Reiki master. This involved a ritual ceremony, where i would be introduced, and opened up, to the life force energy, that fills our entire universe. Once i was attuned, i would be able to channel this life force energy, for the purpose of healing the human body, and also the mind. I started to look for a Reiki master to attune me, there seemed to be three levels of attunement, number one was the basic attunement, an introduction to the life force, if you like, to make sure it was something you would like to do with your life. Attunement two, was the next level, this level introduced the use of the Reiki symbols, to enhance the power, and flow of this life force energy within you. The Reiki symbols also gave you endless options to use the energy in vastly different ways. Attunement three, was to become a Reiki master yourself, enabling you to attune other's. I felt that i just wanted to get started, and get myself attuned. I immediately started to look for a Reiki master locally, at first i couldn't seem to find any Reiki master's locally, then out of the blue, i was driving past a local shop, not too far from where i worked, and i noticed a sign on the side of building, advertising Reiki treatments. I thought, if i could at least get into contact with somebody who did Reiki treatments for a living, they may be able to point me in the right direction, of getting myself attuned, or better still, they may be able to attune me themselves. I took a picture of their sign, on my iPhone, so i could visit their website site later that evening. To my great surprise, on their website, they were advertising training courses in Reiki, and also many other area's of spiritual development. As i continued to read through their very interesting material on their internet page, i became very excited, that i had again found exactly what i had been looking for, and also in a place, that was very close to where i lived. Everything again seemed to be coming together in my life, just at the right moment, just when i felt i needed it the most. I now felt myself to be ready to contact the Reiki teacher's, so i could embark onto the healing part of my life's journey, not really knowing where it would lead me next. To my surprise, when i emailed one of the Reiki teachers, her name was Margaret, i instantly knew she was the one, who was going to attune me with Reiki, Margaret was also my mothers name, this was a very clear sign for me, and i knew that i didn't need to look any further for my Reiki teacher. After two, or three emails with Margaret, my first attunement was set for a few weeks time, i didn't mind the delay, it would give me a chance, to finish my Reiki book, and research this fascinating subject a little further. The weeks seemed to pass very quickly, and i was getting quite nervous, my attunement was going to be done on a saturday afternoon, it was from twelve o'clock, till about five o'clock in the evening. I carried on using my new found healing abilities, all the way leading up to the day of my Reiki attunement. I was not sure if i should mention my new healing abilities, i felt that it was better to go in there, not expecting anything at all. The day of my Reiki attunement finally arrived, i was working in the morning, we were to busy at work, to have any time off. I usually only finished work about twelve o'clock on saturdays, but i knew that i would need to finish earlier, so i could get to my appointment on time, and not be in a state of stress, and rushing. Luckily that day, turned out to be very relaxing, and i did get my chance to finish much earlier than usual. On my way to the attunement, i felt myself getting quite nervous, at what lay ahead of me. I had already read many stories of people going through all sorts of emotional turmoil, after their first Reiki attunement, it seemed like the attunement could possibly bring out emotional blockages, held within the body, and for some people, this would be quite difficult to deal with. I hoped that my previous removal of my emotional blockages, earlier in my life's journey, would put me in good stance, for this attunement ahead today. When i arrived at the shop entrance, there were five or six people gathering out side the premises, even though i didn't know Margaret's face, and we had never met before today, i instantly knew that the lady standing in straight in front of me, was Margaret. I also felt at that point, she also knew who i was. I said hello, and walked past the waiting group of people outside of the shop, i then entered another room filled with another group of people, i was ask to sit down, and would i like a cup of tea, i said i was ok, i had brought some drinking water with me. I sat there with this group of strangers, while they were all talking among themselves, i was then introduced to a lady named cath, i instantly warmed towards this lady, she reminded me, of my late Nan, who i loved dearly. After about five minutes, i seen Margaret approaching, she started to speak to a few people in the group where i was sitting, she then turned to me, i then introduced myself, i explained that i had come for my Reiki attunement, she warmly smiled at me, and said we would be starting soon. Margaret then ask me to follow her, into the next room, i soon realized that there would be two of us, having an attunement today, myself and also another lady, who Margaret already knew, from a previous time before this one. This fact, did not bother me at all, in fact i felt much better, that somebody else new to Reiki, was doing it with me. We both sat down, with Margaret sitting just in front of us, Margaret started off the day, by giving us some folder's containing important information, regarding our Reiki attunement, and also generally information about the history of Reiki, and also its many uses in human, and animal life. We also covered some other spiritual aspects about life, that Margaret was also involved with, including angles, and aura viewing. These subjects weren't new to me either, but i felt, that i did not want to mention this here, i felt that i just wanted to go with this nice flow that we all seemed to have, with each other. I felt a great sense of trust, and peace in the presents of Margaret, it was like i had known her, for such a long time, a very strange feeling indeed. We talked about Reiki for a least two hours, and we also covered, different ways to scan peoples aura's, and energy centre's across the body. We even used dowsing techniques, which i throughly enjoyed. When it was our turn to view each others aura field's, i was in for quite a surprise, when i viewed my partners aura field, i caught a brief glimpse of something, i had never seen before, it was like the human aura field, but much lager in its size. Margaret said to me, that she also seen it, she explained that it was my Reiki partners spirit guide. At first, i didn't know what to make of it, but i had no other explanation for it, at this point in time, so i accepted Margaret's interpretation of these strange events. The time eventually came, when we were both ready for our Reiki attunement. We both sat on two chairs, with our back's to each other, Margaret was going to attune us both at the same time. I knew this was a pretty common scenario, sometimes up to ten people could be attuned at any one time. Two for me, felt just right, we both sat with our eyes closed, waiting for Margaret to perform the attunement. When Margaret started to move her hands over my body, i instantly felt something happening in side of me, i seemed to get a instant rush of energy through my entire body. Feelings of lightheadedness began to set in, at one point, i nearly opened my eyes, in a state of panic, but these feelings began to pass, and i eventually settled down. The whole process only lasted ten minutes, but the after effects were sticking with me, i still felt quite light headed, i also felt very hot, and started to sweat. My Reiki partner seemed to be having a totally different reaction, she was getting quite emotional, and upset from her Reiki attunement, i knew that every body reacted differently, in their own way. Margaret was great, she gave us plenty of support. We all sat there for a while, just having a talk between ourselves, everything seemed to be very peaceful between us. I was starting to feel a great sense of happiness from inside of myself. The time had now come to try our newly discovered Reiki healing powers on each other. My Reiki partner lay on the relaxation bed first, then with Margaret's guidance, i performed my first Reiki treatment. Even though this was my first time for giving a Reiki treatment to somebody, it just felt so natural, and right to me. I also got, a very good reaction from my Reiki partner, she said that she felt very relaxed and clam, she also said that this was quite unusual for her, because she usually finds it very hard to relax herself. I also throughly enjoyed my turn for the Reiki treatment, it was a wonderfully, and relaxing event, i just felt like going off, into a long deep, and peaceful sleep. We then finished off our day, with a good set of hugs between each other, and Margaret said that in the next few weeks, we may go through some changes, emotional, and possibly physical. This didn't bother me at all, in fact i was looking forward to new challenges, and changes that may come my way, over the next weeks, and months of my life. In fact i said to my self quietly, bring it on. At that Margaret made it very clear, that if we needed her for anything at all, we could contact her anytime, which was very nice, and also very reassuring. In the weeks that followed, i noticed my self, reacting differently to many of life's situations, sometimes i would react to a situation totally out of character, other times i would seem to get quite emotional indeed. A few weeks later, Margaret invited me to a Reiki share evening, which i was very excited about. I had been practicing my new gift, beginning to enhance it with some of my own healing technique's, that i had discovered, and also learned from my new book, that i had bought. It was my first Reiki share evening, the idea was that anybody could come to the evening, and have Reiki performed on them by a Reiki practitioner. They could also see, if they would like to learn it for themselves. The evening turned out to be a great learning curve for me, i had the chance to try my healing, on somebody totally new, it felt great. My partner for the night was also fantastic, she was very pleased with the Reiki treatment, that i had given to her, she also said that she may look into getting Reiki attuned her self. I began to love these amazing feed backs, that i was getting every time i used Reiki, they started to spur me on even more, they made me feel extremely happy within myself. It felt like when i was giving healing energy to others, i was also getting healed in some way, my energy levels began to soar through the roof. After the Reiki share evening, i ask Margaret when i would be able to do my level two Reiki attunement, i felt that i was ready. Margaret said, that it was best to wait a least a month or so, before moving onto my next attunement. I totally understood, and set a date in four weeks time, i knew that it was best to wait, but inside, i was hungry for more. In the weeks that followed, my Reiki energy seemed to be flowing with much greater intensity, i was performing a treatment on my son, and half way through the treatment, i started to see spinning vortex's on his body, very faint at first, but they were definitely there. I knew from my studies, that these were the energy centre's of the body, and i was very lucky, and privileged, to be able to see them, with my own eyes. I also noticed, that i could seem to spin them, with the palm of my hand's. My son also said that he could feel me doing this, especially around is stomach area. The four weeks to my next Reiki attunement, seemed to fly by, before i knew it, it was upon me. I was very excited by what lay ahead before me, i had already felt the big changes that the first Reiki attunement had brought into my life. At this time i could only wonder what gifts, the next Reiki attunement would bring into my life. It was the day of my attunement, i had butterflies in my stomach, i eventually arrived at Margaret's house, where the second attunement would be carried out, this time i would be doing the Reiki attunement alone, with no Reiki partners. I felt this was the best way for me, i could totally concentrate on the task's in hand. Margaret greeted me as usual, with great warmth, and comfort, i instantly felt totally settled in her strong presence's. We got to work, with learning the Reiki symbols, these symbols, and their meanings interested me greatly. You could either draw these symbols in the air to activate them, or you could just visualize them, before using them. Visualization was perfect for me, i found this method a lot easier, i seemed to be very good at visualizing anything i put within my mind's eye. Once i had learned the Reiki symbols, we then covered their meanings, and different uses, within Reiki healing. The time eventually came for my attunement, i again sat on a chair, then Margaret performed the second Reiki attunement. I again felt the strong activation of my energy centers, inside my body, these energy centre's in the body were called chakras. I had already read deeply on this subject, so i was well prepared for their activations, during the attunement. This time i did not seem to get the light headed feeling at all, i just felt warmth, and very peaceful feeling throughout the whole process. My second chakra, or third eye energy centre, was very active during the attunement, it had also been quite active for a few weeks, prior to the Reiki attunement. I still don't know the significance of this, it seems my third eye has been very active, nearly all the way through, my life changing journey so far. When the attunement had finished, we sat and talked for a while, then Margaret introduced me to earth crystals, this was the first time, that i had really thought about crystals, in the respect of healing, anyway. I had already bought a crystal from Margaret's shop a month or so earlier, but this time was very different, Margaret introduced me to the real power, and also the energy of earth crystals, for the purpose of healing, and also meditation. I lay down, and started to relax, Margaret then laid a crystal grid formation around my entire body, this consisted of fifteen different crystals, lay in a grid like formation. The effects of this crystal grid on me, were truly dramatic. Margaret left me to relax, for about thirty minutes or so, during my meditation, i had very vivid visions, much like dreams, i felt that the crystal's, had put me into a trance light state. The feelings i felt were one of deep pleasure of some kind. I felt like i didn't want to awake from this deep meditative state of mind. When Margaret eventually re-entered the room, i just about managed to bring myself around form the trance like state, that i was in. I explained to Margaret, that i had seen things, while i was in my deep meditative state of mind, she didn't seemed surprised at all, by what i was telling her. It was as though she already knew, what i would go through in these deep, trans like state's of mind. We finished off the day with a Reiki treatment on each other, then i left for home, to see my family. I felt that i had gone through a great change, in just a few hours of my life. When i eventually arrived home, i tried to relax, and also take in everything that my body had just gone through, and was also about to go through. But i was also looking forward to the new beginnings, and discoveries that lay ahead of me, Thank you Margaret.

CHAPTER 28

Healing, and Discovering the Healing Power of Earth Crystals

With my recent introduction, to the healing art of crystal grids, i felt driven to better understand their powerful and mysterious uses, for the healing of our human bodies. I decided that i would embark on a new quest to enlighten myself in this magical, and secret art of crystal grids. I found out immediately, that these beautiful crystal's were formed over many thousands of years, by this amazing planet we call home. This meant that these magical crystal's contained the very building blocks of our entire planet, and also the universe at large. I believe that they hold, within their very structures, some of the many secrets to life itself, i also began to discover very quickly, that their use, along with Reiki, could make them an extremely powerful healing combination. I was very lucky, that Margaret had given me a crystal gift, after my last attunement with her, i immediately started to use, and study its many uses. I quickly found that crystal's, and meditation were a gifted combination. The crystal's seemed to enhance the meditative state greatly, at time's, even sending me into a trance like state of mind. I wanted to grow my crystal collection immediately, at this time, i only had a few in my collection, these were the ones given to me by Margaret. She was very kind, and had given them to me, on my last Reiki attunement, with her. In the days that followed, to my astonishment, i discovered that my daughter Danielle had been collecting many different crystal's over the early years of her life. I obviously did remember buying her the crystals, over the years, but never thought anything more about it. She had not bothered with them for many years, they were all stored away in a case, that she was given many years before. I ask my daughter Danielle if i could have her crystals, because of my new found interest in earth's different crystals. She was very happy for me to have them, she said that she would find them the next day for me. The very next day, to her word, she had found her collection of earth crystal's. When i opened the box, there were more than thirty different crystal in her beautiful collection. The quality of the crystal's were outstanding, my daughter had truly looked after them well, i promised my daughter Danielle, that i would also treasure her crystals, and give them the best care possible. Now that i had discovered the crystal's true power in our earthly lives, i wanted to put them to use, in every area of my life. I couldn't believe that these amazing crystal's had been with my family for so long, right under my nose, just waiting to be re-discovered, when i was ready to use them in my life. I started to use many types of crystal grid's, i even started to use my own patterns, with great success. I found that certain crystal's, would affect me in totally different ways. The one area, that i placed the crystal's on a regular basis, was my third eye area. Sometimes the crystal's would project vivid images into my mind's eye, it was like watching a movie, of flashing images. Most of the time, the images didn't seem to make any sense to me, but sometime's i would get very meaningful images, ones i could relate to, in my current life. I started to carry certain crystal's around with me, this was very useful for protection, from negative energies, that i would sometimes come into contact with, in my many daily life experiences. I found that certain crystal's would absorb, the negative energy, so it would not be able to attach itself to me. The weeks that followed, i acquired some rarer earth crystal's, giving me a chance to experiment with their powerful, and different kind's of energy. I now use earth crystals on a regular basis, for both healing, and meditation. I have found them to be an invaluable tool, in both area's of my life. If you feel yourself drawn to any types of earth crystal's, please don't pass them by, they may hold invaluable information, relating to your life. I also know, once you have felt their amazing energies, you like myself, will want to explore these fascinating healing devices, in much greater detail.

CHAPTER 29

Healing Path continued, Reflexology, Indian Head Massage, Aromatherapy

In the weeks after my second Reiki attunement, my physical body, and my spirit, seemed to be uniting into one again. I now feel that, we are born into this physical world, with our body, and spirit, totally as one, joined into one harmonious being. But as we grow, and come into contact with many of life's daily challenges, we begin to separate from each other, turning into two different entity's, which in turn only leads us into pain, illness, sadness, and a whole array of other negative situations, in our daily lives. Only when we begin to reconnect with our true self, do we fully begin to heal ourselves, and also begin to re-discover, the true wonders that life holds for us, here on this planet. I now feel that i am starting this journey of reconnection, bringing balance, and happiness back into my life. I now feel that i fully understand the road that i must journey down, to fully reconnect to my inner self. I feel that i am only at the beginning of my Life's journey, but i feel that this journey as already brought me, great happiness, peace, and many other different treasures, that life has decided to show me, along the way. I could only of dreamed, about these many new feelings, that seem to be entering into my life, on a daily basis, i feel that i have grown immensely in the last two years of my life's journey, bringing me to a point in my life, where i truly feel that i understand, my purpose for being here on this planet. I have continued to practice my new healing skills, with great enthusiasm, then to my great surprise, i was guided to another fascinating healing technique, called reflexology. This involved the massage, and manipulation of certain points on the feet, and also the hands. This would then elevate certain health problems, around the body. I was introduced to reflexology, through a chance meeting with friend, that i had not seen for a very long time. I was immediately hooked, reflexology seemed to go very well with Reiki, they seemed to go hand, and foot with each other ha! ha!. I started to home study reflexology, with great interested, i quickly purchased some book's on the subject, and also gathered a lot more fascinating information from the internet. I began to treat myself with reflexology, also incorporating Reiki healing with it to. The effect was dramatic, the relaxation i began to experience was again totally life changing in every way. I then, began to use both of these healing technique's on my family members, which also produced fantastic results. These new studies, and developments in my life, were taking me closer, and closer to my inner self, beginning to reconnect me to my true self, and life purpose here on this planet today. I was eager to learn more, and more, then out of the blue, i received an invitation from the local colleague, asking me if i would be interested in taking a five weeks introductory course, in reflexology, body massage, aromatherapy, and also indian head massage. I was stunned that i had again, been guided to the next step in my life's journey, it was unmistakable, i knew it was my next step in my life's journey. I immediately signed up for the five week course, i couldn't wait to learn more about these fascinating healing, and relaxation techniques. My first lesson was upon me, i felt quite nervous, i knew that the course was filled with female students only. But i kept my faith, and to my great surprise, the course tutor was a man. This immediately put me at ease, in my new learning environment. I felt that i was silly to be nervous, about being the only male student on the course, i made friends with everybody there straight away, i found it great fun, and also a very relaxing environment for us all. The tutor was fantastic, he teached the lesson's, with a sense of fun, combined with new discovery. I loved every one of the lessons that he gave to us. I began to look forward to the next weeks lesson, with great anticipation, about what i would learn next. We got to practice our new skills on each other, over the five weeks course, i began to get some great feedback, on my new skills, from my practice partners. This again, began to give me great encouragement, even my class tutor, thought i had previous massage experience. I was also surprised to find out, that my tutor had very similar interest's in life to me. He was also a Reiki healer, and practitioner, yoga trainer, and he also practiced meditation on a regular basis, just has i did. I knew then, that i could learn a great deal from this very interesting man. Over the last weeks of the course, i listened to him with great interest, picking up on any pointers, or guidance that he may be unwittingly giving me. The last few weeks of the course, brought us into the realm of indian head massage, and also aromatherapy, both subjects were truly fascinating to me. I began to learn about both subjects at home, and on the course days as well. I also purchased my own aromatherapy kit, for me to use at home, while doing my own healing. By the end of the course, i felt that i had gained a wealth of new healing techniques, and knowledge that would send me further down my road of new discovery, in the arts of healing the human body, and also the mind. I also felt that i had made some great new friends, on this amazing course, they all seemed to have very similar interests to myself. This was a great new experience for me, meeting like minded people, seemed to give me a sense of normality again. When the course finally finished, i couldn't help but feel a small sense of loss, i wanted it to carry on for much longer than it did, i felt i was learning so much from it, but i knew that it could not go on forever, and i would just have to wait for my next pointer, in this amazing life's journey so far.

CHAPTER 30

The Five Tibetan Rites

I feel that i must finish my book, with a fascinating new discover of something really special. I have been introduced to a book in the last few months, called Ancient Secret of The Fountain of Youth, by Peter Kelder. This book describes five simple exercise's developed by Tibetan monks, many centuries ago. These five Tibetan Rites as they have come to be known, are believed to hold the secret, to human ageing, and wellbeing. These five exercise's are performed in a set sequence, they are believed to rejuvenate our ageing bodies, by bringing in new life force energy, re-sparking the vitality of life within us. When i first read these word's, i have got to say, i was quite skeptical to say the least. But i knew that over my life's journey so far, i have been guided to many different books, all seeming to give me many different answers, in many different way's, to some of the many pressing questions about life itself. I knew that this book was no different, and i had been guided to it, for a reason, so i began to read through the entire book in just one night. I was intensely intrigued by its magical, and mystical contents. Once i had completely familiarized myself, with all of the five different exercise's, i then decided to try them for myself, to help me feel, and see the results for myself. I then began to incorporate them, into my daily life exercise routine, at first, i started with only doing five or six of each different exercise, they looked very easy at first, but they definitely seemed to activate, the heart, and muscle's around different area's of my body. I felt quite at home with the five exercise's, i found them very similar to my yoga exercise's, i hoped, and also believed, that this would give me a little bit of a head start in learning, and also practicing these exercise's in my daily life. I began to practice them, first thing in the morning, i found it quite easy to fit into my morning routine's, it usually only took me around twenty minutes or so, to complete the five exercise routine. As the weeks went by, i started to increase the repetitions of each exercise, my aim was to get to the maximum repetitions the book recommended, which was twenty one of each different exercise. I found that after about a month of doing the five Tibetan Rites exercise's, my strength, and stamina greatly started to improve in all area's of my body. By this time, i was also able to do the twenty one repetitions that the book described, and also recommended you work yourself towards. In the later weeks, i was also able to do them much faster than before, i noticed that i was starting to loose weight around my abdomen area, i was actually getting my six pack back. This felt amazing, i looked ripped, and lean again. I felt i had much more energy, i started to look forward to doing my five rites every morning, it didn't at all feel like a chore of any kind. Before this i usually thought that bodily exercise's always felt like hard work, but these exercise's were totally different. In the months that followed, my body changed further, i lost more weight, and seemed to gain more muscle mass, and strength, in every area of my body. This may sound silly, but i found that the little ache's we all seem to get from time, to time, seemed to disappear. At first i never even noticed it, i seemed to take my new found health for granted at first. I also noticed that, i wasn't catching cold's, like the rest of my family members, and the time i did actually catch a cold, it seemed to clear totally in a day or so. It may sound strange, but i was actually feeling much younger, and vibrant again, this felt amazing because i was actually approaching my fortieth birthday. I started to think to myself, this could be actually working, i also began to notice that the grey facial hair around my face was beginning to disappear, not totally, but there was a definite improvement. Many people started to ask me if i was dying my hair, which i wasn't. I felt truly excited inside myself, it was like the excitement of a child discovering something magical, and new in their life. From this point on, i have not missed one day of the five Tibetan Rites exercise's in three whole months, and i knew it was beginning to show, in every area of my body, inside and also outside. I started to pass this book around to different people that i knew, hoping that they would have the faith to believe, and start to use this magical information for themselves. I now also share this information with you, the reader of this book, hoping that you will also discover what i have discovered in these last months of my life's Journey. This new found energy, and vitality i have discovered has also helped me on my healing journey, i feel much more energy inside of me, giving me the opportunity, to channel more life force energy, into the people i treat, and heal. I now look forward to a life filled with health, vitality, and mystery. I now feel that this is the perfect ending to my book, i hope this book, has filled you with magic, wonder and also inspiration, filling you with a new sense of inner discovery, about life itself.

FINAL WORD'S

I truly wish with all my heart, that the readers of this book, are enlightened the way i was, with the discovery of life's many gifts, and hidden secret's. I hope i have revealed to you, in the many pages of this book, some of the many secret's, to our human existence, here in this vast universe. My hope is that this book will truly enlighten you, and begin to open up your heart, and mind, to the many magical part's of our earthly lives, here in this vast universe. I feel that somewhere along our human evolutionary path, we have forgotten many of these true treasure's, that life holds for us all. I can only hope that this book, will give you a glimpse into some of these special, and also magical parts of life, that i feel sometimes remains hidden, from the vast majority of people on our planet today, God bless you all, with all my heart. Before i write the words, The End, i would like to say thank you, to my family for their special support, through my life's changing journey, and for putting up with the many changes, that i have gone through, over the past three years of my life. I must also say a special thank you, to my amazing mother Margaret, for her constant help, and support with the writing of my first book.

The End.

Author

P J Nicholls

Please feel free to contact me, with any comments, or Question's
Contact Information:
Facebook Philip Nicholls,Warrington, Cheshire
email nico2007@talktalk.net